PISTOLS TO PRESS:

Lessons on Communication from an FBI Agent and Spokesman

Steven,
all my best,
Jeff Lanza

By Retired FBI Special Agent
Jeff Lanza

Communication Dynamics Publishing
Mission, Kansas

Published in the United States by
Communication Dynamics, LLC.

ISBN 978-0-615-45459-7
Printed in United States of America
Cover design by Melanie Rutherford
First Edition

Opinions expressed in this book are entirely those of Jeff Lanza and not those of the FBI.

To Pam, my wife, and our two children,

Christopher and Angela

Contents

Introduction

During my twenty-year career as a Special Agent for the FBI, I had the delightful opportunity on many occasions to speak to groups about my job. Whether they were kids or adults, the audiences that I spoke to always had a lot of questions. In fact, three of the most common questions which I was asked over the years were these:

"Have you ever been shot?"

"Have you ever shot anyone?"

"Did J. Edgar Hoover really wear a red dress?"

Permit me to answer these questions, in case you were wondering. The answers, in order, are:

No, no, and no comment.

Well, actually these weren't the most common questions, but they have definitely been asked. And since you will be reading in this book that you should never say "no comment," my answer to question three is also no. The story about J. Edgar Hoover, who was the Director of the FBI for 48 years, has been widely discredited, as it came from a mob associate and convicted perjurer who was most likely attempting to undermine the FBI's credibility.

I loved talking to groups about the FBI, and in 1990 I learned something else that I could talk about. I received a phone call from a person at FBI Headquarters in Washington, D.C. who told me that the badge I carried had also been carried by Agent Frank Smith, who was present during the Kansas City Massacre in 1933. This was a historic event in law enforcement history which gave rise to the modern FBI. I was deeply honored to carry this badge throughout my FBI career.

I was honored again in 1990 when I was assigned the collateral duty as a spokesman for the Kansas City Division of the FBI. Geographically, this responsibility extended over a swath of land that covers all of Kansas and about two-thirds of Missouri. It was a busy place for law enforcement. The next eighteen years provided me with an inordinate number of opportunities to work with the press and to learn many lessons on communication.

Notice that I didn't say lessons on communication with the media. That would be too restrictive. Media communication is a large part of my experience, but the lessons described in this book can be applied in a general way to various types of communication across many industries and professions. They can be used for internal and external communication; in corporate America, non-profits and government; by executives, managers, front line employees, human resource professionals and, of course, law enforcement professionals.

There are especially important lessons pertaining to crisis situations. How an entity experiencing a crisis is perceived in the long term is often dependent not on the crisis itself, but rather on how information about the incident is communicated to various stakeholders, including employees, customers and the general public. This is of particular importance in an age where traditional journalists no longer totally control the flow of information about an incident. You don't need a degree in journalism, a satellite dish or a newspaper production facility to convey information to the public. Essentially, all that is required to communicate knowledge (be it right or wrong) to large amounts of people are a cellphone and a thumb.

As for media communication, there seems to be no shortage of preventable errors in how information is communicated to the press. Communicators who treat the media like an enemy, who lack preparation or vigilance, who make impromptu comments or who show little or no empathy to the plight of their audience are just asking for communication failure. If there was any doubt whether or not Tony Heyward, the former CEO of BP, should have kept his job following the crisis at Deep Water Horizon, that doubt, as well as public confidence in the company, was removed following his comments about the disastrous oil spill caused by his company. He showed no empathy to the people affected by the crisis ("There is no one who wants this over more than I do. I would like my life back"). He also tried to minimize the gravity of the situation ("It's relatively tiny compared to the very big ocean").

Humanizing your organization with a sincere display of empathy before you begin to tell them what you know makes it easier for an audience to accept your further communications. Teddy Roosevelt captures this sentiment perfectly with the quote, "No one cares how much you know until they know how much you care."

We have all seen examples where impromptu comments can have a lingering aftereffect on a community. Recently, the Sheriff in Polk County, Florida was asked by the press why his deputies had shot a man sixty-eight times. His response: "Because that is all the ammunition that we had."

In 2010, we saw the Toyota Corporation break a basic rule of good communication by not being the first and most credible source of information about their crisis with faulty accelerator pedals.

Sometimes, even when people think they are doing the right thing, they take it too far. A colleague of mine in New York City told me that the head of the New York FBI field office had once come up with what he thought was a great sound bite for a press conference that had do with a criminal case against some mob figures. The FBI agent told the press that "the FBI is twisting the tourniquet on the tentacles of organized crime." The metaphor might have worked, except that an Associated Press reporter wrote his story with the FBI agent quoted as saying, "The FBI is twisting the tourniquet on the testicles of organized crime." That is a metaphor most would choose not to envision.

I can point to the mistakes of others, but I too have pulled some big ones in my time and learned some important lessons in the process. This book is about those experiences and others I have had in working with the media for eighteen years. It is my desire that this experience and these lessons will help you in becoming a more effective communicator.

Chapter 1

Pistols to Press

A person watching nationally televised commercial programming on a Sunday evening in 1968 between the hours of 8:00 p.m. and 9:00 p.m. had three choices: *The Ed Sullivan Show* on CBS, *Disney's Wonderful World of Color* on NBC and *The F.B.I.* on ABC. My choice at age eleven was to watch men in really nice suits catching bad guys, week after week, in sixty-minute episodes based on real FBI cases. I wanted to be just like them, nice suits included. In one episode, the show's central figure, FBI Inspector Erskine, played by Efrem Zimbalist, Jr., returned a kidnap victim safely to her overjoyed parents. The idea of being in an occupation that provided that type of reward thrilled me, and it sparked my interest in becoming a FBI Special Agent.

My attraction to a career at the Bureau continued to grow long after the last of *The F.B.I.*'s two hundred and forty-one episodes aired. I earned my undergraduate degree in Criminal Justice, but when I graduated, I had not met the minimum age requirement to be a Special Agent, which is twenty-three. I continued in school and earned a Master's Degree two years later, at which time I met the age requirement, but did not have the required work experience (which is two years for someone with a graduate degree). So I entered the corporate workforce at Xerox Corporation, doing a job I really enjoyed as a computer systems analyst. But I never took my eyes off the Bureau.

My corporate career at Xerox offered good pay and many opportunities for advancement. But it just did not offer the possibilities and excitement of the job I dreamed of as kid and the opportunity to save kidnapped children, investigate the mafia or to go undercover. (Not to mention the nice suits).

During my time at Xerox, I paid attention to news about the FBI, and my interest in a career as an FBI agent was further enhanced by stories about important FBI cases and the high-profile arrests they made of mobsters and other thugs. In early 1987, I decided to see if I could fulfill the dream that was sparked by a television show many years before. So, I walked into the local FBI office and applied to be an agent.

Almost one year later, after numerous interviews, an extensive investigation into my past, a battery of fitness tests and a probing physical exam, I received an offer of a position as a Special Agent for the FBI. A few weeks after that, I walked into the door at The FBI Training Academy in Quantico, Virginia to begin new agent training.

My training began on a Sunday evening in February, in a classroom with fifty other men and women, collectively labeled as New Agent Class 88-5, which indicated that we would be the fifth group of new FBI agents to graduate in 1988. Shortly after 8:00 p.m., we all raised our right hands and swore to protect the Constitution of the United States against all enemies. After completing the FBI oath of office, we sat down in our chairs and began three months of training after which we would officially be issued a badge and a gun and receive orders to report to one of the fifty-six FBI field offices in the United States. As I sat down, the thought entered my mind that during that same hour, on a Sunday evening in 1968, exactly twenty years prior, I had been watching *The F.B.I.* on television and dreaming of the moment that this would happen.

***

New agent training at the FBI Academy consisted of many hours of classroom training on such topics as organized crime, drug cartels, undercover operations, white collar crime, counterintelligence, counterterrorism, interviewing and interrogation and a plethora of other topics that we would need to know in order to carry out our mandate as federal law enforcement officers.

Outside the classroom, we spent many hours in defensive tactics training, preparing for confrontations and arrests. In the gym we trained physically for the FBI fitness test, which required that each of us, in order to graduate, meet certain standards in various physical endeavors.

On the gun range, each new agent in training fired over four thousand rounds of ammunition using various weapons on which we needed to be proficient in order to become an agent. We would be issued a gun to carry with us at all times while on-duty.

About halfway through the training program, a much-anticipated day arrived. It was the day all of us were going to be issued our official orders assigning us to one of the FBI field offices in the United States. The standard protocol was to have agents begin their careers in one of the forty-four small-to-medium-size FBI offices (measured in number of agents). Unless you wanted be assigned to one of the twelve biggest FBI offices, you had absolutely no choice in where you would be sent. If you preferred a big city, such as New York City, Washington, D.C., or one of the other larger offices, you were allowed to list these cities in your order of preference. Their high cost of living made them more difficult to staff, so the Bureau was happy to take volunteers for these cities. Most agents, however, preferred to begin their careers in smaller cities, where a lower cost of living made life on a government salary more acceptable.

A young lady and future agent that sat next to me in our classroom at Quantico was a New Yorker through and through. She grew up there, her family was there and she couldn't imagine living or working anywhere other than the center of her universe. Besides that, she wasn't about to let somebody she didn't know at the FBI decide where she was going to live and work. So naturally, she listed New York City as her number one choice for assignment and fully expected to receive her orders to that location, as it was the most difficult FBI office to staff.

The FBI made a big to-do of the whole process on the day agents got their orders. Each person, one at a time, was called up in front of the entire class and handed an envelope containing an official letter which designated the person's field office of assignment. Each person had to first tell the entire group where they thought they would be assigned and then open the envelope and read their actual designated office of assignment.

In the case of our new agent class, the day we each learned about our office of assignment happened to occur on April 1st. As I waited my turn to receive my orders, the New Yorker who sat next to me was called up and handed an envelope. Her smug expression indicated that she thought the pomp and circumstance was unnecessary in her case because, perish the thought of another place, she was going to be assigned to New York City. Stating what most of her classmates had heard many times before, "I think I am going to be assigned to New York City," she opened the envelope with a barely perceptible eye roll, indicating her boredom with the inevitability of the whole affair.

She pulled out the letter and started to read. "I have been assigned to…," there was two seconds of silence before she continued, "LITTLE ROCK!" At this point it sounded to me like she used a profanity, but I couldn't tell for sure because of the collective mixture of an empathetic groan and laughter coming from the class.

There is nothing wrong with Little Rock; it is just that she had her heart and mind set on New York City. She dejectedly walked back to her seat next to mine. She turned in my direction and asked, "Where the hell is Little Rock?"

"I believe it is outside of the New York metropolitan area," I responded.

In retrospect, it didn't surprise me that our class counselors used the opportunity to pull an April Fool's Day joke on the New York trainee. What was remarkable was that they let the joke go on for so long. Several other agents were called up to get their orders while she sat next to me and visibly stewed. Finally, they called her back up and gave her official orders to New York City, much to both her relief and mine, because I had to sit next to her until graduation, still six weeks away.

When my name was called to go up to the front and announce my orders, I said I thought I was going to be assigned to Knoxville (just a wild guess). I opened the envelope and read, "I have been assigned to Kansas City." Immediately I heard an eruption of applause from two people in the class who were both from the Kansas City area. "Jeff! Kansas City! Alright!" one yelled out, still clapping for me. I wasn't sure what to think, but since these guys were clapping I thought I should clap myself. So I walked back to my seat applauding that I had been assigned to Kansas City. A few seconds after I sat down I started to think, *what the heck am I clapping for? I don't want to go to Kansas City.*

I may not have known it at the time, but Kansas City turned out to be a great place to work, live and raise a family. I joined the FBI with the anticipation that I would be carrying a pistol, working undercover, investigating the mob or finding kidnapped kids. I never imagined that some of the greatest satisfaction I got in my job would come from working with the press. A unique set of circumstances in Kansas City gave me the opportunity that I may not have had in other FBI offices. At that time I received my orders, I had no way of knowing this, nor did I have any knowledge about the history of the FBI in Kansas City.

I got my first glimpse of what Kansas City might be like about a week after getting my orders. One of the FBI class counselors, a veteran agent who had been assigned to several offices around the country during his career, said to me, "You are going to like Kansas City." I asked him why that would be the case, expecting him to say that the city had a low cost of living, that people there had strong Midwest values, or something along those lines. Instead he said I was going to like Kansas City, "because they have some great organized crime there."

"That's fantastic," I replied, not thinking that "great organized crime" in a city really wasn't a good thing. For me, it was a positive because I wanted to investigate the mob. When I arrived in Kansas City, I realized that my counselor's information was a little out-of-date because most of the big mob figures in town were already in jail as the result of an FBI investigation into the mob's skimming money from Las Vegas casinos. I was disappointed that the organized crime work in Kansas City was no longer "great".

The investigation that put those mobsters in jail was a historic one in Kansas City. It broke the back of the mob in the Midwest and evicted them from Las Vegas, which opened the door for the corporate mob to move in there.

The Kansas City mob had been pretty clever in siphoning off money from the casinos. But by the time I began working in Kansas City, the smart ones were in jail and all we were left with were the mobsters that lacked basic common sense. There was a legendary phone conversation which two mobsters had on a phone line that was wiretapped by the FBI. The mobsters, who I will call Tony and Joe, had this conversation while an FBI agent listened to the wiretap:

Tony: Joe, I am really glad you called.
Joe: Yeah, why?
Tony: I got a little problem. I think the FBI is tapping my phone.
Joe: What are you going to do about it?
Tony: I already got it taken care of. I got a new number.
Joe: OK good. Gimme the number.
Tony: I better not give it to you on the phone. I'll meet you for lunch and give it to you then.
Joe: I can't meet you for lunch.
Tony: OK, I'll give it to you now on the phone...but I better give you the number...backwards.
Joe: Good idea.

Tony proceeded to give him the number backwards. The FBI, of course, sent the backwards number to its cryptology department immediately. Six months later we had the new phone number figured out. Well, it didn't take quite that long.

There was another situation involving a wiretapped phone line with which I had first-hand experience. I had been assigned to a white collar crime squad, and one Friday afternoon an agent from our organized crime squad came over to the white collar area. "Anybody want to go on a search warrant on Sunday morning?" he asked. "We need another person."

As a new agent, I wanted to do everything, so I was quick to respond. "Sure, I'll go," I answered.

Two days later, the agent and I arrived at the home of a bookie and served the warrant, which allowed us to take any property believed to be connected to illegal gambling. I was at the bookie's desk gathering the evidence, while the other agent was interviewing the bookie in another room.

It was a Sunday morning during football season, and one might expect what happened at the bookie's desk. The phone rang. I was a new agent and not sure if I should just let it ring or not, so I asked the other agent. "Go ahead and answer it," he said.

Before I tell you what transpired next, I must digress. My father was a small business owner in Norwalk, Connecticut. He owned a Hallmark Card store and a convenience store that was named Jet Variety. As a teenager, I helped out my dad around the store after school, on weekends and during summers. On occasion, a group of men would congregate in the store after buying a newspaper called the *New York Post.* This paper was very popular among the men because it had an extensive sports section. Included in this section were the betting lines for games taking place on any given day. The men would come into the store on a regular basis, grab the paper and talk to each other about what games they were going to bet on that day with their bookie. There were many occasions over the years when I heard the men's conversations and I started to learn about the meaning of the betting lines. Over this time, I learned the vernacular and the parlance of gambling by listening to these men.

About fifteen years later, in Kansas City, I was at the bookie's desk wearing my gun and badge, gathering the betting records in fulfillment of the terms of the court-ordered search warrant. When I asked the agent what to do about the ringing phone, he told me to answer it. So I did.

I answered the phone as I would have under normal circumstances. "Hello."

"Who is this?" The caller asked.

"Jeff." I was not acting in an undercover capacity, so I told him my real name.

"This is Mike," he said.

"Hey Mike."

"What is the spread on the Chiefs today?" Mike asked.

I knew exactly what to tell him because the bookie's paperwork was right in front of me. I knew how to read the lines because it was part of the jargon the men used in my dad's store. I learned it from them and knew how to answer the question the caller had asked me.

"The Chiefs are plus 6 ½," I told him, reading directly from the bookies sheet.

"OK, gimme fifty on the Chiefs," Mike instructed.

"You got it. Anything else, Mike?" I asked, jotting down his bet.

"That's it for now," he replied.

I went back to making an inventory of the bookie's papers when the phone rang again. "Who's this?" the caller asked. A pattern was starting to develop.

"Jeff. Who's this?"

"Frank."

"Hey Frank, what can I do for you?" I asked.

"What's the over on the Vikings?" Frank asked.

Remembering this terminology from listening to the guys in my dad's store, I looked for Vikings on the bookie's sheet and saw the number indicating the total number of points a bettor thought would be scored by both teams together. The bettor could place a bet the final score would be under or over that number.

"Forty-four," I told him.

"Give me the over for twenty-five," Frank said.

"You got it, Frank," I said.

"Thanks Jeff," Frank said.

This went on for about an hour and no one asked why the regular bookie wasn't answering the phone. That is, no one except the FBI agent at our office downtown who was listening to the bookie's phone, as our wiretap on it was still active. I was so new in the office that he didn't even know my name. "I was wondering what the hell was going on! Two FBI agents go in and bust the bookie, and then some other bookie named Jeff starts taking bets," he told me later. "You sounded like a real bookie."

The agent might have been wondering about me, but the bettors didn't. Mostly, they just wanted to get their bets placed. One bettor was also concerned that he might not be able to collect from me if he won his bet. "Jeff, I don't know you," the bettor said. "But I get paid on Tuesdays. You are still gonna pay me right?"

"Yeah, don't worry about it." I said.

"OK. I just want to be sure." He then went on to tell me his name, spelling his last name out letter by letter, followed by his address, with the street also spelled out. "You're gonna come over on Tuesday, right?" he asked.

"Oh, don't worry. We'll be over," I said.

A little later a bettor called who was more circumspect than the previous callers. "Who's this?" he asked.

"Jeff."

"Jeff who?" the caller asked.

I really wasn't that comfortable in this impromptu undercover role as a bookie. His question put me on the spot. I didn't want to give him my last name and I wasn't quick enough to make something up. So I told him the truth. "Jeff with the FBI," I said.

After saying that, I thought I would hear a click on the other end of the phone line. Instead, I heard hearty laughter. "Jeff with the FBI. That's really funny, Jeff with the FBI," he said, cracking up. "OK, Jeff WITH THE FBI! I want a hundred on the Chiefs," he ordered, still laughing.

My time as an FBI bookie came to an end after about two hours of taking bets. What I learned from that experience was that I really didn't think I could be an effective undercover agent. In this situation, I mostly told the truth. In a real undercover case, I would have to learn to be deceptive and think quickly in potentially dangerous situations. I decided to leave the undercover work to someone else.

***

I was getting a little bit bored with white collar crime cases and started looking for other opportunities to serve the Bureau. Undercover work was out, though, and all the good mob cases were already finished. I started to look at ancillary duties, and what came to mind involved the press. Each FBI field office had a designated agent who spoke with the media. I thought that working with the media would be interesting but I was too new at that time to apply for that job, not to mention that it was already filled by someone else. However, I had shown some interest in the position and an opportunity presented itself which allowed me to test my capacity to work with the press.

A television show called *Unsolved Mysteries* was profiling a cold Kansas City FBI case, and they needed an agent to go to their studio in Los Angeles when the show aired. The agent was needed because, after segments about unsolved cases aired, the show provided a toll-free number that viewers could call if they had any information about the case. A phone bank had been set up for the show, with operators ready to take calls after each episode aired. The producers of the show wanted an investigator standing by the phones in case the operators received a call that looked it might result in a promising lead.

The case that was being profiled involved the murder of a teenage girl in 1970. Evidence connected her boyfriend to the crime and he was charged with her murder. He fled the area and became a fugitive before the police had a chance to arrest him. Twenty years had passed and, in all likelihood, the boyfriend had crossed over state lines in order to avoid being arrested. That gave the FBI the authority to open an unlawful flight to avoid prosecution investigation, which allows the Bureau to use its nationwide resources to assist local police in the apprehension of a fugitive.

This case was not just cold, it was frigid. The FBI agent in charge of the fugitive investigation was happy that the case was being profiled on the show, but he was unable to go to Los Angeles to talk to callers with good leads. Having expressed an interest in working with the media, I was asked to do it in his place.

You might imagine that with millions of viewers, you would get a lot of phone calls with useless information. This case was no exception. One particular call stuck out in my mind as being a very low priority lead for follow-up. The caller had been watching the television game show *Jeopardy!*, which aired immediately before *Unsolved Mysteries* in the caller's area of the country. Having watched both shows, the caller was absolutely convinced that one of the contestants on *Jeopardy!* was the fugitive murderer. Wasn't that a coincidence, I thought. The man had been a fugitive for twenty years and he happened to be both a contestant on *Jeopardy!* and the subject of a profile on *Unsolved Mysteries* on the exact same night.

There were a few other leads, but none that resulted in the criminal's arrest. Sadly, it is still an open case today, over forty years after the murder.

Even though this remains an unsolved case, the experience of working with *Unsolved Mysteries* gave me an idea of the media's power in helping solve crimes as well as a taste of working with the press. I decided at that point that I would apply to be an FBI spokesman when the job became available. When that time came, I assumed the additional responsibility of working with the press while continuing my regular case load as a pistol-toting Special Agent.

Chapter 2

The Sound Bite

For many years as a kid I dreamed of being an FBI agent because I thought investigating crime would be much more rewarding than other occupations. In my television-influenced mind, I perceived the FBI as the crème de la crème in law enforcement. So I set my aspirations high. When I became an agent, I did not imagine that I would do anything else but investigate crimes. But the FBI offers many collateral jobs which support the Bureau's overall mission. These jobs are filled on a volunteer basis by agents who do the extra work along with their investigative duties. Agents take on jobs such as firearms instructors, defensive tactics trainers and evidence response specialists, among other things. There is no additional pay for these responsibilities, only additional work, but it is work that agents love.

One of the collateral positions in every FBI office is the media coordinator, better known as the spokesperson. It is a job I held for eighteen of my twenty years as an agent. The media often contacts the FBI because they are gathering information to do a story about a crime or an incident such as a bank robbery, an anthrax threat or a missing child. Sometimes reporters catch wind of a sensitive white collar crime or other type of investigation that is not supposed to be known publicly. They might then call the FBI to confirm the existence of a Bureau action or official investigation. When a member of the news media contacts the FBI for any reason, they must talk to the FBI media coordinator. At other times, the media coordinator contacts the press in order to publicize surveillance pictures or other information about a crime which may generate a tip or lead that might help solve a case.

The media coordinator keeps busy with these requests from the traditional news media in addition to the calls for FBI-related information of a general nature from authors, bloggers, screenwriters and others. In most FBI field offices, the media coordinator keeps fairly busy just handling the press on a day-by-day basis. In some of the bigger FBI offices, such as New York, Los Angeles and Miami, there are multiple media coordinators who work full-time as such.

The Kansas City FBI office, for most of the years I worked there, staffed one media coordinator and one backup. Neither were full-time jobs. The agents or professional support staff who handled the media relations work had other responsibilities as well. During most of my career, I investigated white collar crime while also serving as the media coordinator.

During my new agent training at the FBI Academy in Quantico, Virginia, we were told to anticipate the possible presence of media at places where the FBI would be conducting investigations. Most commonly, the media would be outside a home during the execution of a search warrant, at an office during a hostage situation or at the scene of a bank robbery, but they also popped up at numerous other places where the FBI was present. "Your job investigating crimes will sometimes intersect with the media's job to report on crimes. If the media shows up at a crime scene and asks you a question," the instructors at Quantico admonished us, "tell them that you work for the FBI and that you are at the scene in your official capacity. Any further information, if provided at all, must be released from the media coordinator. If at any time you get a phone call from a reporter, don't answer any of their questions. Instead, refer them to the media coordinator."

The rules were made very clear to us early in our training. The FBI has a very tightly controlled media policy which dictates that only the media coordinator and management staff are allowed to speak to the press. The reason for this policy is to prevent the release of information that may cause harm to an investigation or damage the reputation of a person who is the subject of an FBI probe. Many cases which the FBI investigates, especially in the area of white collar crime, do not result in charges being filed. Public knowledge of a person or business being investigated by the FBI can sometimes damage reputations, even if no evidence is found which results in formal charges.

One of the most vivid examples of this involved the investigation into the Centennial Park bombing at the Atlanta Olympics in 1996. A pipe bomb in a backpack exploded at the Olympic venue during an outdoor celebration one evening. One person died and several were injured. There would have been more casualties, if not for a security guard named Richard Jewell, who told people to move away from the backpack before the explosion.

Hundreds of law enforcement officers from numerous agencies began an investigation to determine who was responsible. One theory of the crime included the possibility that Jewell himself was the guilty party. Word about this was leaked to the press, which widely publicized his suspect status. As it turned out, Jewell was cleared of the crime, but his reputation was damaged severely by the coverage.

FBI policy is not the only restraint on employee communication with the media. Federal laws have been enacted to protect the rights of individuals who are investigated by the FBI. These privacy laws make it a federal crime for someone to release information about an investigation, unless it results in the filing of charges. There are exceptions to these laws and procedures, but for the most part, a newly trained FBI agent leaves Quantico for their assignment in one of the FBI field offices knowing that they are not allowed to speak to the media. This was not a problem for me, as I had no desire or intention to ever do so. However, this changed about one year after I arrived in Kansas City.

The Kansas City FBI field office, like many around the country, has criminal investigative responsibilities categorized into squads. These squads are made up of teams of agents who focus their investigative work on a specific type of criminal activity. Most FBI field offices have squads that investigate terrorism, organized crime, drug crimes, computer crime and many other types of illegal endeavors. When I arrived in Kansas City, I was assigned to a white collar crime squad. I assumed the decision was made to put me there based on my education and prior work experience. Unlike many agents hired by the Bureau, I am not an accountant or an attorney, but I hold a master's degree in business administration and had worked in a white collar job for Xerox Corporation for seven years prior to joining the FBI. I became the newest agent on the white collar crime squad. I was joining a group of men and women, a few of whom had taken a cut in pay to become agents. It was clear from my conversations with these agents that for them, as with me, it had been difficult to give up a good salary and the perks of the corporate world, but becoming an FBI agent had been a lifelong dream, the achievement of which made the loss in income much more palatable.

About a year after I began my career at the FBI, an agent entered the white collar crime squad room. He had recently been appointed as the backup media coordinator in Kansas City and was working with a local television news station on a story about white collar crime. "You have had some high profile cases on this squad recently. A reporter with the local NBC station wants to do a news story about white collar crime," he said.

"A television story about white collar crime, now that's exciting news," one of my squad mates said.

"Maybe they will start a TV series about accounting fraud," another agent blurted out.

I didn't know much about television news at that point, but I knew enough about white collar crime investigations to agree. Some television news programs advertise their show as "action news." White collar investigations were about as far removed from any discernable action as you could get. White collar crime, which is characterized by fraud, concealment or deceit, is very interesting to investigate, but these cases are extremely methodical and slow-moving by nature. I couldn't imagine that a news program could make anything about white collar crime seem exciting enough to attract and hold a television viewer's attention.

We learned that the reporter wanted to make the story personal, with the agents as the focus. His emphasis would be on why agents were motivated to join the FBI and what was driving them in their effort to lock up white collar crooks. The media coordinator knew that I was the most recent agent to leave the corporate world, and he thought I might provide an interesting perspective. He asked me if I would consent to be interviewed for the television news segment and I agreed.

The next day, a reporter and a cameraman came into our squad for interviews with me and a few other agents on the squad. The reporter wanted me to explain the reason I left a job at Xerox Corporation with lucrative pay and great career advancement opportunities to become an FBI Special Agent.

During the interview, which was being taped for later broadcast, the reporter sat directly in front of me. The cameraman was to the left, videotaping me at a slight angle. The media coordinator was to my right, sitting next to the reporter, staring at me while I answered the reporter's questions. I understood that he was there to monitor the interview and to make sure I didn't say anything that shouldn't be broadcast to the public, such as a reference to a current FBI investigation.

The problem for me was that he did more than just monitor the interview for inappropriate comments. The cameraman signaled he was rolling videotape and the reporter asked me his first question. The media coordinator stared directly at me and cocked his head slightly to make sure he heard my answer. Through his facial expressions, he gave me real-time feedback as I spoke to the reporter. I felt as if each word I said was being instantly analyzed. Each time the reporter asked a question, I could see the media coordinator out of the corner of my eye, eagerly waiting to hear my response. As I spoke after each question I could see by the look on his face that I wasn't doing a good job answering the questions. It was easy for me to tell how the media coordinator felt because as I spoke, he winced. The longer my answers went on, the more he winced.

I was trying my best to respond in an articulate way to the reporter's questions about why I left Xerox to join the FBI, but in the middle of my responses, the wincing would begin. I wasn't sure why my responses didn't meet with his approval, but the wincing bothered me so much that at one point I just stopped mid-sentence. As I was saying, "A career in the FBI investigating crooks provides much more personal reward than I could ever have received in a corporate job...," I stopped before elaborating on the comment and turned my eyes to him, "What's wrong?" I asked.

"That was good," he said.

"What was good?" I asked.

"What you just said…that was good," he said.

"Why were you giving me that funny look? You know, you were wincing at me."

"That's because your answers were OK, but too long. I know you are trying to answer the questions, but you need to be more concise. The last answer you gave was good."

The reporter smiled, as he knew the media coordinator was trying to get me to talk in a sound bite for television. "We can work with that, you are doing fine," the reporter said.

A sound bite is usually less than ten seconds long and is inserted into a news segment to provide information and reinforce the point the reporter is trying to make in a story. A standard local news story, which runs about one and a half minutes during a thirty-minute newscast, contains a beginning and an end, which is usually done by the reporter. In between are four or five sound bites from people that have something to add to the story. In television news parlance, this is called a package. The sound bite is an integral part of the package. Without the sound bite, there is no package.

When I responded to the reporter's questions, I was providing an answer that took between thirty and sixty seconds for me to complete. There is nothing wrong with doing that. In fact, most reporters want to hear your entire answer so they can understand your position and the facts of the situation in a meaningful way. However, if you take that long to answer a question for television news, which is what I was doing in my interview, you can guarantee that your response will not air in one continuous piece.

The production of local television is based on the short attention span (be it real or perceived) of the television viewer. The reporters and editors produce stories in such a way that no single image appears on the screen for more than ten seconds, and in most cases less. That time frame applies to both the image of a person being interviewed and the associated sound of the person's voice. The term "sound bite" refers not only to the voice of the interviewee but the video as well. When a person has a message to deliver in a taped television interview, they have about ten seconds to do it.

Some people might say that it is difficult or even impossible to deliver a message in ten seconds. I believe this is plenty of time to deliver a message, as long as you construct your thoughts and form your statements with the sound bite in mind. If you don't do this, and instead take thirty seconds to answer a question, your response will be cut up into smaller segments of ten seconds or less. It is possible that none of those segments, standing alone, will convey your point. The statements might not be used at all. In some cases, what does end up in the story may seem as though it has been taken out of context.

The problem for me during my interview about white collar crime was that I was not thinking with a sound bite mentality. The reporter needed the background (my full response) so he could understand the reason why I joined the FBI, so there was no issue with explaining that fully. However, when you give a full explanation, it needs to be summarized and amplified in a statement that lasts no longer than ten seconds. That is the sound bite.

If you are going to do a television interview, you should have a "made-for-television" sound bite for each of the key points that you want to get across to the reporter. Give full answers to each question, but try to include a sound bite at the beginning or end of each answer. Make sure that you pause for a second in between the full answer and the sound bite so the reporter will have a clean editing point when he or she prepares the segment for television.

In my interview about white collar crime, I gave the full answer, but I was not talking in a way that could be used to summarize my comments well in the sound bite format. The media coordinator instinctively knew that what I was saying was going to be edited to the point where it would not reflect its intended meaning. That is why he started to wince as my comments went on. When I stopped in mid-sentence because of his wincing, what I had actually done was create a sound bite with a clean editing point.

When the story aired, that sound bite was the only part of my interview that was included in the package. It was the portion of my statements that had summarized and amplified my message about why I left Xerox to join the FBI. It took less than ten seconds for me to say. The news segment turned out very positive and I learned a great deal about television news just from doing that interview. Overall, I was impressed by the reporter and the work of the media coordinator in helping him "coordinate" the FBI resources for the story. The winces made me very uncomfortable, but I still felt that I wanted to be the FBI spokesman someday.

A few months later, I was eating lunch with the wincing backup media coordinator, when he said, "I have been transferred to New York."

The New York City Division of the FBI was the Bureau's largest in terms of agents and support personnel, and because of the high cost of living in that area, it was hard to keep staffed. Agents were routinely transferred there from other FBI offices, and he became the latest from our office to receive his orders to go there.

After my experience involving the television news story about white collar crime, I thought I might volunteer to be the media coordinator, but it was too soon. I had only been an agent for a little more than a year and I did not have enough experience in that capacity, not to mention any background or experience with the media aside from the interview I had done about white collar crime a few months prior. If I was going to volunteer for the job, I thought that I should at least have more time as a street agent, or I wouldn't have a chance to get it.

Following the agent's transfer to New York, the backup media coordinator job was filled by a female agent on the white collar crime squad. She excelled at the position and I figured she would be doing it for a while. But a few months later she too was transferred to New York, and the position came open again.

It was time for me to make a career choice. If I took the public relations path as a collateral job, I would never be able to work in an undercover capacity for the FBI. Once your face is on television, working undercover becomes dangerous. This is especially true today, in a time when the Internet and YouTube make television appearances permanent. Even in 1990, news programs could be recorded and replayed. An undercover agent could get exposed years after a television appearance if the target happened to see him or her in one of these recordings.

In any case, I was ready to give up undercover opportunities following my impromptu experience as an undercover bookie. After that incident, I had made the decision that I probably would not want to be an undercover agent. Although it was exciting and interesting work, I felt uncomfortable in that role.

In making a career choice, another factor I considered was my squad. White collar crime investigations have propensity to move at a snail's pace. However, we had our share of excitement on a regular basis investigating corruption in Kansas City. My squad specialized in investigating allegations that kickbacks or bribes had been solicited by politicians.

During the early 1990s, the squad was having a field day investigating crooked politicians. At one point, several members of the Kansas City, Missouri City Council had been officially charged with violations of federal law. The Mayor of Kansas City was asked by a newspaper reporter how the situation might affect the public's perception of his administration. He said that the city's problems, "Could lead voters to think less of politicians." Trying to put a positive spin on the issue, he added, "That the majority of the city council has not been indicted." Technically speaking, if he was referring to a two-thirds majority, he was correct. We had, however, indicted a simple majority of the city council.

This was an exciting period to be involved with white collar crime investigations and I found this work to be very rewarding. But working with the media gave me the opportunity be involved with many more cases which our office was investigating, at least from a public relations standpoint.

One day, after much consideration, I walked to the other side of our building and asked to see the Special Agent in Charge (also known as the SAC) of the Kansas City FBI. He happened to be in his office at that moment, and after a few minutes I was called in to talk to him. In retrospect, if I had written an official memo, he would have taken the time to review my credentials for the job and probably would have denied me the position due to my lack of qualifications. But, because I was talking in person to the man calling the shots, we were able to discuss the issues face to face in real time. It wasn't easy.

I told him I was in his office to be considered for the media coordinator position. His look told me that I had violated the chain of command protocol taking this action, but he was a nice guy and wasn't about to throw me out of his office. "What type of qualifications do you have for the job?" he asked.

I was silent. While I was trying to come up with something that might apply, he spoke again, "Do you have any experience in journalism?"

"No."

"Do you have any experience in communications?"

"Not really."

"How about public relations, done that at all?"

I knew I had better come up with something fast or I wouldn't have a chance at the position. At the time, I was taking a night course on creative writing at a local community college. This was the only bone I had to throw at him. So I thought I would give it a shot and told him about the course.

"No experience in PR, but I am taking a night course about creative writing."

After a few seconds of silence he said, "Creative writing.....OK, we'll give you a shot."

Just like that, I had the position and was allowed to talk to the press. Creative writing may have played a role in getting the job, but I knew from my limited experience that being successful at it was going to depend not as much on creative writing, but rather, the ability to tell the truth under potentially adverse conditions. And maybe a creative sound bite or two.

Chapter 3

Preparation

"I don't know." These are three words many people are reluctant to say to a reporter. I can understand that some people don't want to appear unknowledgeable or unprepared to talk about a subject, but if you don't know the answer to a question, saying that you don't know is simply the best response. You can always offer to find information or refer the reporter to someone who might know the answer. But never try to camouflage your lack of knowledge by giving a response that you are not sure is correct. In short, don't BS a reporter. Doing so could spread false information and make you look bad when reporters find out the truth, which they have a way of doing. Providing inaccurate information can also destroy your credibility, the most important asset you have. Whether your audience is made up of the media, your employees, your customers or any other party that has a vested interest in what you have to say, if you lose your credibility, you will lose your ability to lead them through a crisis. It will serve you well to follow a cardinal rule of crisis communication, which is never to lie or mislead.

Many times, you can avoid the predicament of not knowing an answer to a question through good preparation. Generally, the 80/20 rule applies when preparing for a presentation, speech or media interview. You should spend about 80% of your time preparing and 20% doing. For interviews with reporters, it is wise to gather as much information as possible about the issue at hand before the interview takes place. This may require you to question people who have the information you need to prepare. Asking questions and listening well are part of effective preparation. Never be reluctant to ask questions, no matter how simple or basic. Don't be afraid to be a pain in the neck to someone when it comes to gathering the information you need to prepare for an interview.

I became practiced at this while I prepared to talk to the media about the most common federal crime that garners media attention: bank robberies. Kansas-City-area banks were held up about once per week on average, so I got quite a bit of experience in gathering and disseminating the information the media needed to report on the heists. Most of the time the process required me to talk to agents on the bank robbery squad to obtain the basic information a reporter needed to write a news story: the who, what, when, where, why and how of the events. The agents were always very willing to provide me with information because they knew that publicity often led to the identification of a suspect, making their job a lot easier. But the process did require me to be a pain at times, often to multiple people. If four agents responded to a bank robbery, the responsibilities to investigate the crime would be divided among the group. For instance, one agent would interview the teller that was robbed, another might interview a witness in the parking lot, yet another might gather information about the monetary loss from the bank president, and so forth, until the investigation at the scene was complete.

To get accurate information about the crime, I would sometimes have to talk to three or four agents who had information I needed. Many times I would be trying to gather the information about the bank robbery while they were still investigating what had happened at the bank. They would be conducting interviews at the bank, obtaining the suspect's mug shot at the police station, working with our photo specialist to print pictures from the bank surveillance camera, or even heading out to another bank heist. My job was to provide accurate and timely information to the media about the robbery, and this often required me to interrupt these agents to obtain the information.

One of my biggest concerns in providing suspect information to the media was that it would prove to be inaccurate. I envisioned myself being called up to the witness stand during a trial of a bank robber and being asked by the defense attorney, “Isn’t it true, Agent Lanza, that you were quoted in *The Kansas City Star* saying that the suspect in the bank robbery was 6 feet, 2 inches tall?” I would answer yes, and the attorney, just like on television courtroom drama, would ask his client to stand up before the jury so they could see with their own eyes that he was 4 feet, 8 inches tall. Fortunately, nothing like that ever happened, despite the fact that witness descriptions sometimes varied widely.

My job was to ask a lot of questions, sort through the information and figure out what I could say to the media that would help reporters do their story and help us solve the crime. It never really bothered me to ask questions because I wanted to be clear on the information I needed to do my job.

Much of my preparation for handling these communication challenges came from my childhood job working in my father’s convenience store in Connecticut, where we moved when I was twelve. I think I learned a great deal from working with customers. The store was very busy at most times, with many repeat customers buying newspapers, cigarettes, lottery tickets and general convenience items. There was a lot of small talk with customers and I learned to communicate in a friendly and outgoing way. I think these people skills helped me when I became an agent, and especially in dealing with the press as a spokesman. When I became an FBI agent, I tended to treat people like customers. This engendered relationships which went a long way in helping me get what I needed to do my job, whether it was a criminal confession or a positive news story.

In my dad's store I also learned to ask questions when necessary. As a young kid, I really didn't know too much about working in a retail operation so I had to ask a lot of questions to do my job. There was one occasion that I will always remember when I asked the wrong question at the wrong time. After school one day, I was working in the store stocking inventory and I opened a carton of items to be stocked on the store shelf. The carton contained six tubes of an item in yellow and blue boxes with which I was not familiar. I looked for a location to place the items on the store shelf but there were none in stock, so I had no idea where I was supposed to place the inventory. I was standing about ten feet down the aisle from the cash register, where about six people were standing in line to check out. The store manager was ringing up customers. I was very anxious to finish my work, and I didn't want to wait until the people cleared out to ask for guidance as to where on the shelf to put the item. I held up a tube in my hand and interrupted the manager by yelling out, "Hey, where does this go?"

Momentarily diverting his attention from a customer he replied, "What is it?"

I looked at the tube again to make sure I had the name right and yelled, "Preparation H!"

His response was delayed only long enough to give the six people in line, none of whom could hide the amused looks on their faces, time to turn around and look directly at me. I knew I was soon to be embarrassed by the words that were to come out of the manager's mouth because at that moment I remembered that the product was a treatment for hemorrhoids. The manager excused himself from the customers and walked gleefully in my direction. With the pretense of politeness, he leaned over to whisper in my ear. Only he wasn't getting ready to whisper the answer. He wanted to make sure everyone in the store could hear the punch line. So he answered the question loudly: "Up your ass!"

Technically, he was exactly right, according to the instructions on the tube, which I later read. This little episode clearly made the manager's day, as he repeated the story over and over again to customers. At one point he added to my humiliation by asking me to reenact the whole thing for one of his friends. Needless to say, it was a long day at my dad's store. At least I knew that in the future, it was unlikely that I would be *that* humiliated by asking a question.

Despite my embarrassment, I was not sorry for trying to get information I needed to do my job and neither should you, especially if your job is to communicate vital information to key audiences. To help you remember this point, just think of Preparation H. If your "preparation" is done well before you talk to a reporter, your employees or anyone else, you will likely have the information people want, be able to answer their questions and be satisfied with the result of your communication.

It is also important that you don't go overboard on the information that you communicate, as I once did. Strangely enough, this situation also related to hemorrhoids.

Chapter 4

The George Brett Incident

If you have prepared properly before you communicate with an audience, you will have collected a large amount of information that you are ready to impart. This doesn't mean that you have to provide every bit of it to your audience. Verbally dumping the entirety of the information you have accumulated during your preparation process can lead to a failure to communicate the key points to your audience. This especially applies to public speaking. Too much information can result in background "noise" that may cause your key messages to be lost. Keep your messages clear, concise and to the point.

A few years ago, when I was introducing a speaker for a local group, my introduction became a mini-speech in itself with an unintended ending. I belong to a breakfast club, which consists of about 100 people who get together once per week, have breakfast and hear a person from the community speak for about 20 minutes. One week I had the opportunity to introduce a person I had asked to speak at the club. The person was George Brett, the Hall of Famer and former Kansas City Royals baseball player.

I knew Brett because his kids and mine went to the same school. We also coached our kid's baseball team together when our sons were in first grade. I have been a huge baseball fan since childhood, and have always rooted for the New York Yankees, longtime rivals of the Royals. Even though Brett was a Royal his entire career, it didn't stop me from admiring his great abilities as a baseball player.

Brett had a very high-profile career with many accomplishments. The one that is most memorable to me was the season he had in 1980. He came very close to hitting .400 that year, a feat that had not been accomplished since 1941 (and still has not been repeated). In fact, Brett was so close, that all he needed was five more base hits during the entire season to finish the year at .400. Batting .400 means reaching base by a hit 40% of times you are at bat, which is a remarkable feat over the long baseball season, during which a player comes to the plate over 500 times in twenty-six weeks.

The Royals made it to baseball's World Series that year and played the National League champions, the Philadelphia Phillies. As the culmination of the baseball season, the World Series and its subsequent crowning of baseball's best team is a huge media event. There is unbelievable pressure for the players to succeed against the fiercest competition on a world stage. A lot is expected of all the players, and in 1980, even more was expected of Brett because of the great season he was having.

Amidst all the hype and hoopla and unrelenting media coverage of every issue and development surrounding the series on and off the field, something happened that no one could have anticipated. The star player of the Kansas City Royals, George Brett, removed himself from the second game of the World Series. The problem was extremely personal. Brett had a case of hemorrhoids. It was a bad enough case, the world was told, that Brett just couldn't play. In what became the world's most famous case of that particular affliction, he had minor surgery and returned for the rest of the series.

Brett is such a class act that his accomplishments on the field that year far outweighed any embarrassment that the incident might have caused. Brett hit over .300 for the Series but Royals ended up losing to the Phillies in six games.

Brett retired from baseball in 1993 and was elected to baseball's Hall of Fame by a unanimous vote the year he was first eligible, in 1999. That was only appropriate since he is truly one of the best baseball players of all time.

So when it came to the day that I was going to introduce Brett to my breakfast club, I wanted to do it well. Since I coached kids' baseball with George and had asked him to speak to the club, it was my privilege to introduce him and I wanted to honor his major accomplishments on the field, of which there were many.

Just as I would do before a television interview or speech, I prepared for a mini-speech to introduce Brett. I researched all of his accomplishments on the field. He led the league in hitting in three different decades. He was voted baseball's most valuable player three times. He hit a key home run against the New York Yankees in the postseason playoffs. Etc. There were too many achievements to remember, so I made bullet points for notes, which filled-up two index cards. There were so many accomplishments to mention, and I didn't want to leave any out.

As I started to read down the list of bullet points at the breakfast, the introduction was starting to get long, especially since the person I was introducing was only going to talk for 20 minutes. I wanted my introduction to be comprehensive, which was a mistake. I should have stuck to one or two key points and then brought the main act on stage. But I didn't do that, and since the introduction was so long I wanted it to have its own grand finale. I thought I would wrap it up by saying that Brett missed hitting .400 in 1980 by just five base hits. Then I was going to say to the audience, "Please join me in welcoming George Brett!"

The problem was not *how* I prepared to introduce Brett, or even that I over-prepared. What became an issue was that I tried to include it all. That was my first mistake. I started my introduction by telling people we met through our kids' school, and how I had been a big fan of his. Then came the statistics. I realized after a few mumblings about batting titles and home runs that the audience was getting antsy and that I was talking way too long. They came to hear him, not me! *Too much information. Should have narrowed it down to a couple of points.* These thoughts ran through my brain as I looked down at my second note card, which had even more points to cover.

At this juncture I had two options: I could have just stopped and brought him up, or I could have speeded up my introduction to get through it faster. I chose to speed it up. That was my second mistake. The longer it went on, the faster I talked.

As the introduction mercifully drew to a close, I had one more thing to add about Brett's flirtation with the .400 mark. What I meant to say was this: "…and in 1980 George gave the country a thrill by coming very close to hitting .400. In fact, he was only five hits shy of hitting .400 that year." But at this point I was talking very fast and starting to slur my words a little. As a result, what came out of my mouth was this: "…and in 1980 George gave the country a thrill by coming very close to hitting .400. In fact, he was only five shits shy of hitting .400 that year."

The room erupted in a deafening roar of laughter. If anyone thought I had said it on purpose, they were very wrong, since I could never have planned anything that would make people laugh *that* hard.

The laughing had barely subsided when Brett took to the floor. He didn't miss a beat: "Well, come to think of it, 1980 was the year I had hemorrhoids…so I probably was five *shits* shy of hitting .400."

More unrestrained laughter followed as I slinked back to my seat. The embarrassment I experienced reminded me of the day in my dad's store when I asked where

Preparation H goes. I guess I have a way of embarrassing myself with issues about hemorrhoids. Brett followed with a fine talk to the group and I apologized to him later for the misspoken words.

I learned from this incident that in most instances, good communication is clear, concise and to the point. During your preparation process, it pays to gather all the information you can by asking good questions of the right people. Consult written and online sources as necessary. But don't feel that you have to provide all the information you have collected. Too much information becomes noise that can actually distract from your communication. It is a good idea to be cognizant of the information if you need it. But you should take the information you have and organize it into three of four clear and concise points that can be used for broadcast sound bites or as key points for a live audience to remember. Most people won't remember more than that anyway and key points are what you need for an effective broadcast interview.

As for the Brett introduction, I learned that shorter is better, mainly because the audience was there to hear him, not me. Since the embarrassing incident, I have made sure to keep it short. On the flip side, I make it easier for people who are responsible for introducing *me* as a speaker by helping them get to the point and not belabor my introduction. Groups that have asked me to speak get a full copy of my biographical information to use as they wish for background or to promote my speech. However, I don't want them to use all of that, or even large chunks of it, to introduce me. When I arrive at the venue to speak, I find the person who is going to be introducing me and hand them a copy of my business card. On the back there are printed three concise points I want them to say in my introduction. It takes them less than 30 seconds to get through it before I come on stage. This technique has worked like a champ every time. The introduction is short and to the point. I like it, the introducer likes it, and the audience does too. And it is especially nice because my introduction does not, *at any point*, make reference to hemorrhoids.

Chapter 5

Vigilance

Have you ever heard the statement, "Don't worry about it, it's not the end of the world"? Did you ever wonder what you would do if it *was* the end of the world? What if you were asked to discuss the end of the world on television? Reporters can sometimes have a funny way of phrasing questions, and on one occasion, I was asked to talk about the "beginning of the end of the world."

I have found that successful communication is often dependent on the vigilance of the communicator. Being vigilant means being careful – and watching out for techniques that journalists employ to obtain information from you for a story. Some issues of importance in this regard are: the lead, live microphones and cameras, the "dead air snare" and off-the-record comments.

The lead: During live television interviews, to avoid being taken off guard, it is important to be prepared to handle any type of question, no matter how it is put to you. Prior to live interviews, I find it very useful to get a copy of the script the anchor will read while introducing me and my interview. When a guest is brought into a news program for commentary, there is always a segue to that guest. This segue is a transitional statement that introduces the issue at hand and the credentials of the interviewee, helping the audience understand the content of the story.

For live television, this transitional script is usually read by the news anchor immediately before the interview begins. In most cases, the script is written by a producer in a way that is intended to maximize viewer interest and keep them tuned in. If the story has built-in conflict, there is no need for creative writing to generate interest. Using a teleprompter, the anchor reads the facts at hand and follows by saying something like, "Here is John Smith to tell us more about it." What comes next is a series of questions by the anchor and answers by the guest, after which the anchor sums it up and moves on to the next story.

What the anchor reads tends to set the stage for the interview. With this in mind, it is very important for you, the guest, to know what the anchor is going to say because it reveals the focus or angle of the story. This knowledge helps you formulate an appropriate response. If what the anchor says is accurate and has been stated well, you can agree with it to reinforce the point and then proceed with answering questions. However, if the introduction is incorrect, contains embellishments or presents the situation without context, your first job is to set the record straight and provide that context. In order to do this, you should ask the anchor how they will introduce your segment and be listening to what they say as your interview is about to begin.

An even better method is to get the script and review it beforehand. Since the text read by the anchor on a teleprompter is written in advance, you should review the script which will be used to introduce your segment. How do you get this? Simply ask for it from the person who has escorted you into the television station. Take time to review it so you can be ready to respond on point. If you see that they are setting up your interview in an undesirable way, you will at least have time to contemplate their angle and to prepare an effective response.

On one occasion, during a live interview on local television, this practice demonstrated its usefulness. This situation occurred in late 1999 when I was asked by the local FOX affiliate to come on their morning show to talk about what the FBI was doing to prevent a terrorist incident at the dawn of the new millennium. There had been a great deal of press up to that point which speculated that terrorists were going to strike the United States at the stroke of midnight on January 1, 2000, theoretically because they had been "called" to do so at this significant time.

I agreed to discuss the issue on the news program and I arrived at the station in plenty of time to get situated and wired up without rushing. The person who had connected my earpiece and microphone handed me the script for my segment. In my mind, I expected to see something along these lines:

"There have been reports that terrorists are planning to strike at the dawn of the new millennium. Here to talk about what the FBI is doing to prevent a terrorist strike is FBI Special Agent Jeff Lanza."

However, as I read the script, I was taken aback, "The dawn of the new millennium has brought reports of an apocalypse. The Bible mentions a sacred area in the Middle East where the final battle between good and evil will be fought, signaling the beginning of the end of the world. Now, here in our studio is Jeff Lanza to talk about it."

My interview was about one minute away and I thought, "Wow, they want me to talk about the beginning of the end of the world!" This was an area that was clearly not part of my expertise. At that point I did the only thing I thought was appropriate: I made a joke of it by saying, "I have done a lot of interviews over the years and this is the first time I have been asked to discuss the beginning of the end of the world."

The anchor laughed and said, "Well, let's hope that doesn't happen."

I can only assume the scriptwriter for that segment wanted to add some drama into a story that was rather mundane, because most of what the FBI was doing was behind the scenes and couldn't be discussed on television. You should always be prepared for the insertion of some conflict into a story if no obvious conflict already exists, and plan for how you might deal with it.

More and more, it seems the media must have conflict in every news story, presumably to compete with other forms of entertainment for viewers. In the FOX segment I was on, they really kicked the conflict up a notch. What could be more compelling than the battle between good and evil with the world at stake?

Live microphones and cameras: Anytime you are in the presence of a reporter, keep your guard up. Don't say or do anything that you wouldn't want to be broadcast or reported. There have been many instances of people getting burned by live microphones and cameras. Even experienced professionals make mistakes. One high-profile example of this occurred during a local newscast on the ABC television network in New York City. The anchor was reading the teleprompter, introducing a segment and the reporter covering it, Mara Wolynski, who was going to speak to the television audience from her desk in the studio. A camera had been broadcasting the anchor straight-on as she read the introduction. Suddenly, there was a switch to another camera and the television viewers saw Wolynski from the side. She didn't know she was on camera, and as the anchor continued to introduce the segment, Wolynski could be seen having an animated conversation with someone off-camera. She was clearly upset with this person and was making angry faces at them. Just before her segment was about to begin, she abruptly ended her communication with the off-camera person by raising the middle finger on her right hand in their direction. You can probably imagine how Wolynski must have felt when she was told her gesture was witnessed by a live television audience.

Hoping that the FCC would have a sense of humor when they reviewed the incident, one of the anchors closed the newscast by saying, "Well, as Mara Wolynski would say, we're number one."

This incident illustrates the point that you should always be vigilant when you are around a television camera. If the professionals can get burned, it can happen to you too, so be careful.

One thing in particular that can lead to trouble is when you lower your guard. Most people have their guard up and are very careful what they say when a television camera is pointed at them and recording their statements. There is a tendency, however, to lower your guard when the camera is pointed away. This sometimes comes into play during recorded television interviews.

If you have the occasion to be interviewed on videotape for a television news program, you will most likely be given a wireless microphone to place somewhere on your clothing on the upper portion of your body. The transmitter will be attached to your belt or placed in your pocket. It is used to transmit your words to the camera a few feet away, where the audio recording that goes with the video of you talking takes place.

The problem typically arises when the formal interview is finished. After you answer the last question, the photographer usually videotapes a "two shot," sometimes referred to as "b-roll," which is short for "background roll." As this is occurring, you stay in your position, the reporter stays in their position and the photographer moves around behind you to videotape the reporter talking to you. This is done so that they have extra video for the story. They also use it when editing your segment, when they cut your interview into smaller segments to fit in the sound bite format. The "two shot" video is used as a transition in this editing process.

During this time, you may have a tendency to relax and let your guard down because the camera is no longer pointed at you. You must remember, however, that you will still be wearing the microphone and transmitter. What you say at that time will be recorded by the camera, and any statements to the reporter can still be used. Just because the camera is not pointed at you does not mean you are off-the-record. Keep your guard up at this time and stay on message.

The dead air snare: It took over an hour for the people from *Dateline NBC* to set up their equipment in my office at the Kansas City FBI building. In preparing to videotape my interview, the crew of the nationally broadcast news magazine show went through a procedure that was methodical, arduous and extremely slow.

The interview I was doing with *Dateline* was about a Kansas City pharmacist named Robert Courtney. Now in federal prison serving a thirty-year term, Courtney was convicted of crimes related to dilution of prescription medications, including chemotherapy drugs. The patients, who thought they were receiving intravenous injections of powerful cancer drugs, were getting almost pure saline instead. *Dateline* had sent one of their reporters to Kansas City to do a segment on the case.

You might imagine that with the show's meticulous arrangement of indirect lighting, numerous sound checks and multiple applications of powder and minute rearrangements of seating positions, its reporter would be ready to match the high quality of the production with compelling questions, constructed with exact precision to get right to the heart of the issue. He would then, you imagine, be able to report the news story in a special way with a unique angle, different from other news stations and reporters, thus justifying the huge expenditure in time, effort and money to conduct the interview in the first place.

However, I found the questions to be less than compelling. “Have you ever seen anything like this before?”

“Were you surprised when you heard about the allegations in this case?”

After I answered each question, I stopped talking. This would be followed by an extended period of staring and nodding on the part of the reporter. This interview occurred in 2001. By that time I had eleven years of experience in front of cameras and microphones, and I knew that reporters used this technique, which I call the “dead air snare,” to elicit further comments from interviewees. In our culture, we have a tendency to respond to people who are staring at us after we have answered their question. It is almost as if the staring causes us to believe that we have not answered the question at all, or at least not to the full satisfaction of the questioner.

The reporter in this case was just trying to get me to talk. From our mostly one-sided conversation, he would take a few choice sound bites and plug them into his story to make his points. He was clearly going for a statement from me reflecting my shock and awe that this type of crime could have even occurred. However, the most important message that I wanted to deliver had to do with patient safety and not the integrity of the pharmacist. The FBI wanted to make sure that everyone who had received prescriptions from Courtney was aware that they might have gotten diluted medication. My appearance on *Dateline* was intended to help in that effort, so I wanted to make sure that at least one of my sound bites included that message.

It was fairly easy to sense what the reporter was looking for based on his questions about the uniqueness of this type of crime. I didn't want my sound bite to be something like, "The FBI was shocked when we saw the results of the drug test. The thought that a pharmacist's greed could lead him to dilute life-saving medication is unthinkable." This was true and it was what the reporter wanted, but I was afraid if I had given such a statement, it would be the only thing they would use from me. In order to deliver my message about patient care, I looked for a way to incorporate it into the "shock statement."

The dead air snare is traditionally a reporter's tool, but it can also be used by interviewees to their advantage. If you answer a question and the reporter waits for more using the dead air snare, you immediately know that question is important to them and it may be the reason they are interviewing you in the first place. Knowing this will help you craft your answers and messages into sound bites that meet your needs as well as the reporter's.

While there is nothing intrinsically wrong or tricky about the dead air snare, it is a technique of which an interviewee should be cognizant. If a reporter asks you a fair and pertinent question, you should respond with a truthful answer. If an opportunity exists to provide a message, you should include that in your answer. If you have answered the question the best way that you can, you should simply stop talking. Never let a reporter's silent nods or dead stares persuade you to continue to speak. Don't worry about the delay. Eventually they will ask the next question.

The dead air snare is not used during interviews that are being broadcast on live television because, as every reporter knows, silence is not the stuff of good broadcasting. However, silence can be edited out on tape. Therefore, in these types of interviews, the dead air snare might be used to get you to say something valuable to the reporter as you try to find words to fill the uncomfortable silence. My advice is to not talk during this time. Just wait, and the next question will come.

Sometimes the results of the dead air snare can be dramatic. One morning in Kansas City, one of my favorite radio reporters responded to the scene of a house fire. He arrived to find a house that was engulfed in flames. Fortunately, the sole occupant had escaped from the house without being injured.

The reporter interviewed the occupant to determine the cause of the fire. He started with the most general and basic question, "What happened?"

The occupant, thinking that the reporter's question referred to the end result of the fire rather than its cause, responded disdainfully with the obvious. “It caught on fire, can’t you see?”

“I can see that. What happened? How did it start? Do you know?” The reporter clarified his question.

“Cigarette,” the man said abruptly.

At this point the reporter’s instincts told him that silence on his part was in order. The reporter waited more than four seconds in dead silence, staring at the man and holding a microphone in front of his face.

The man’s next response illustrates the value of the dead air snare. The man said, “Alcohol.”

The reporter wasn’t about to say anything at this point. He waited over two more seconds in silence. The man’s next statement told the real story of the fire’s origin. “I passed out in my chair with a bottle of Jim Bean in my hand,” he explained.

The reporter, figuring that pretty much summed it up, spoke again, “My, my, you’re lucky to be alive,” he said.

“You can’t hurt an Irishman,” the man explained.

That is the story of a house fire as it aired on the radio news. You can't make this stuff up. In this case, in addition to being the victim of a house fire, the unlucky man was also a victim of the dead air snare, which provided listeners with the real cause of the fire. This true story illustrates two points. First, you should never keep talking after you have answered a reporter's question. Second, if you are going to burn your house down as a result of your drinking, you should at least try to get the name of the liquor that's responsible correct. The bourbon that he passed out with in his hand is actually named Jim Beam, not Jim Bean.

***

There may be situations when you would like to provide information to a reporter, but don't want to have your name attached to it. There are three different ways to do this, although the terminology used to describe them is somewhat esoteric. It is important to recognize the meaning of these terms and, most importantly, make sure that you and the reporter have the same understanding of how your comments will be attributed. Here are the terms most commonly used to describe various types of attribution.

On the record: Everything that you say can be quoted verbatim and attributed to you. Example: "The FBI is looking for another person believed to be involved in the shooting of the Congresswoman," said FBI Special Agent Jeff Lanza.

On background: Your comments can be attributed, but not to you by name. Usually, a more general attribution that names the organization that employs you will be used. Example: "The FBI is looking for another person believed to be involved in the shooting of the Congresswoman," said a Department of Justice employee.

On deep background: Both your name and your organization are kept out of the attribution. Example: "The FBI is looking for another person believed to be involved in the shooting of the Congresswoman," said a person with knowledge of the situation.

Off the record: In this case, there is no attribution linking you to the information. Additionally, no part of the information can be used by the reporter unless it is obtained from another source. In this case, you will not be named at all in the news story.

Communicating on the record is the best way to do business, and most reporters prefer it that way. There are times when off-the-record comments are appropriate, but they are rare. I am not talking here about a leak of information, which is usually undertaken to expose to a reporter a situation of which the reporter either has none or limited knowledge.

A place for off-the-record comments may pertain to a situation where you feel it would be worthwhile for a reporter to have more clarity on an issue or to have information that can help put a story in perspective, but is not something for which you want any attribution. For example, there was a tragic case the FBI investigated involving the death of a federal judge and his wife. A preliminary investigation revealed that the likely cause was suicide, not homicide, which would have garnered serious and protracted media attention. Suicides are tragic, but they are generally considered private matters and not reported to the extent of a homicide.

I needed to tell the media that we believed it was a suicide but I did not want to be quoted saying that was the case because ultimately that was the responsibility of the county coroner. On the other hand, I did not want the media to expend resources or begin a process of reporting on speculation while they waited for the official cause of death. Pete Williams, an NBC News national correspondent, contacted me from Washington, D.C. about the case. He was ready to board a plane with a television crew if the judge and his wife had been homicide victims. I had met Williams the year before and I knew he had an excellent reputation in the FBI as a fair and sincere journalist. He had my trust, so I posed a question: "Pete, can we go off the record?

"Please do," he replied.

"It looks like the case is a suicide, but I really can't be the source of that information," I said.

"I understand. We are not going to report on this story. But I appreciate you letting us know," he replied.

This was clearly a case where an off-the-record statement was appropriate. Outside of situations rare situations such as this, the most professional way to deal with the media, and the one I recommend, is to be on the record. You should be able to stand by your statements with your name and position attached to your comments.

I never saw reason to talk to a reporter on the basis of "on background" or "on deep background." These are methods for releasing information for which you don't have authorization, so you try to conceal your identity from interested parties, with deep background being a more effective camouflage than background. This type of press communication is most often used by politicos to get information out without revealing a source. Generally, it has no place in a business setting.

Remember that being vigilant is important for successful communication – and to avoid being burned by the media. Being vigilant means being careful with what you say and how you act around the media. It is a good idea to learn the lead, watch out for live microphones and cameras, be cognizant of the "dead air snare" and understand the terminology that reporters use to indicate how your comments will be attributed.

May 6, 1988 was a very proud day for me. Twenty years after watching the television show *The F.B.I.*, my dream of becoming a Special Agent became a reality at the FBI training Academy in Quantico, Virginia.

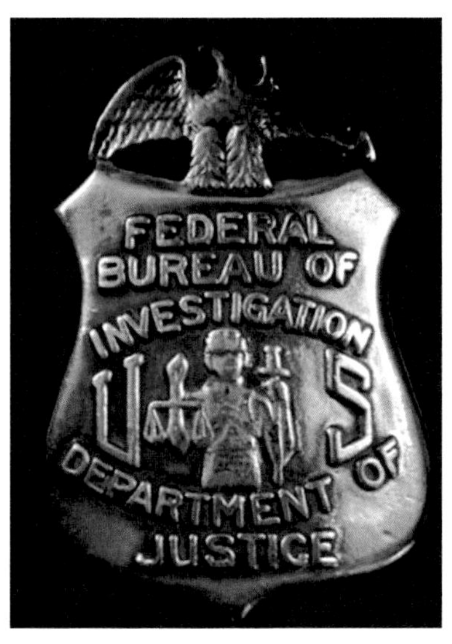

I had the honor of carrying FBI badge number 4920 throughout my career. It was once carried by Agent Frank Smith, who was involved in the Kansas City Massacre. On June 17, 1933, a gun fight at the City's train station resulted in the deaths of FBI Agent Raymond Caffrey and police officers W. J. Grooms, Frank Hermanson and Otto Reed. It was a watershed event which gave rise to the modern FBI.

"Study for 'Over Vitebsk,'" an oil painting by Marc Chagall with an estimated value of $1 million, was stolen from a museum in New York City and recovered about one year later near Kansas City.

I was able to get the excess powder off of my face and clothes moments before I went live on national television with Wolf Blitzer.

The look on my face tells how I felt about the way Connie Chung handled the interview.

The Today Show's Campbell Brown showed incredible sensitivity to issues I couldn't talk about in the case of a kidnapped fetus. Instead, she focused on the elation agents felt when they found the baby alive.

I thought Larry King might begin my interview with a probing question. Instead, his first question was: "Agent Lanza, is this an FBI matter?"

On January 29, 1999 exactly one year after Carlie had been rescued from her kidnappers and safely returned to her mother, the FBI had a birthday party for her. A photographer from *The Kansas City Star* found me holding Carlie during the birthday celebration.

In March 2008, a few days before I retired from the FBI, Carlie, then 10 years old, returned to the FBI again.

Chapter 6

Is this an FBI Matter?

"You are going be talking live with Larry King in two minutes."

That announcement came from a CNN producer in New York City, heard through a tiny device which had been embedded in my ear only seconds before. I sat in a television studio in Kansas City, Missouri, waiting for a live television interview with host Larry King to begin. The producer spoke in such a routine and relaxed way, but I, on the other hand, felt large drops of perspiration accumulating so much on my chest that they would have been visible through my shirt were it not covered by my suit jacket.

For me, this interview was anything but routine, and I certainly wasn't relaxed. I was getting ready to talk about a kidnapping that the FBI was investigating, and I thought it might be a tough interview to handle. After all, this was Larry King who was going to be throwing the questions at me. He had been interviewing people on television for a time not measured in years but rather in decades, maybe even centuries. Nevertheless, I was quite certain that with all his experience, Larry King knew how to handle an interview guest. And that was exactly what I was afraid of: being handled.

In any case, I was concerned that I was going to screw up on live television in front of a national audience. Would I know the answers to Larry's questions? What if I did know the answer to a question but couldn't answer it because it was against FBI policy to answer? If that were the case, would I then look evasive and defensive? What if I said something that I shouldn't have? Would I try to recover from that and dig myself a deeper hole? All these things were whirling around in my brain as I got ready for Larry's first question.

In my mind, the first question was the key. If I could answer that and sound halfway intelligent, I would relax, gain some confidence, and the rest would be a breeze. It was going to be only a short interview, no big deal.

So, my focus turned to the first question. What was Larry going to ask me right out of the box? I had every expectation that it was going to be a tough, probing question contemplated by an experienced interviewer like Larry King and designed to get to the heart of the issue. I thought about all the possible questions he would ask first and how I would respond. As the director gave the ten second warning before my interview was to begin, I was ready. I was mentally rehearsed and prepared for the first question from the venerable Larry King.

He spoke: "Agent Lanza in Kansas City, is this an FBI matter?"

For some reason, Larry put extra emphasis on the word "*this*".

The question was a big softball, which I was not expecting. My next thought was not an answer to the question but rather, "Is that your lead question, Larry? Is this an FBI matter?"

I wanted to say, "Larry, as a matter of fact, the answer to your question is no. You have asked me to be on your show. I am sitting in a studio, doused in face powder, wired up for sound, and a camera is pointed directly at my face for the purpose of bringing my image and voice to the living rooms of millions of viewers all across America, because…it is *not* an FBI matter."

I didn't answer the question that way, but if I had, I would have put an extra verbal emphasis on the word "*not*".

I briefly answered Larry's question, "Yes, it is." I decided not to leave time for the obviousness of my answer to sink in and I immediately moved on to a message. I learned very early in my days as an FBI spokesman, that in a crisis situation, effective communication is extremely important. If you are talking about a crisis, whether you or your company caused the crisis or not, people are going to decide how to respond and feel about the situation based on what you say and how it is said. Ultimately, their feelings about what happened, whether or not they need to take action, whether or not you are to blame for the crisis and whether or not it damages your personal or organizational value in the minds of the audience all comes down to how information about the crisis is communicated.

In this regard I have found that one principle of crisis communication holds true in virtually every instance. People will not remember specifically what the communicator said, but they will remember how the communicator made them feel.

Did the communicator make them feel better, more comfortable, at ease with the situation and how things might be resolved? Did the audience feel as if the communicator was credible, believable, and that he cared about their plight? Or did the communicator make them confused, uncertain, mad or more anxious than they were before?

Ultimately, the goal of a good communicator during a crisis is to make people feel better with accurate and timely information, and to attain a certain level of credibility and trust from an audience. Before this can happen in a crisis situation, people want to know one thing above all else: that you care about them and the difficulty the crisis has caused in their lives. In short, a show of genuine empathy can do some amazing things in the realm of crisis communication. First, it humanizes you or your organization beyond the "talking head." You care, and therefore you become more real than a two-dimensional figure appearing before them on television.

Once people realize that you care about them and the plight they are in, a second transition takes place. They become more open to what you say. Your communication becomes more pertinent because it is coming from a person who cares about them.

After I answered Larry King's question, "Is this an FBI matter?", I felt it was necessary, based on the shocking nature of the case, to deliver an important message to all those who had been affected by the crisis.

The FBI investigation which prompted the interview on *Larry King Live* involved a horrific and extremely unusual crime. A 23-year-old woman named Bobbie Jo Stinnett was murdered in her home in Skidmore, Missouri. She was eight months pregnant at the time of the murder. What made the crime so unusual was that she was murdered for the purpose of stealing her fetus. The woman responsible for the crime, who was later convicted in federal court and sentenced to the death penalty, was named Lisa Montgomery.

Montgomery strangled Bobbie Jo to death, removed the unborn fetus from her body and, after cutting the umbilical cord, got into her car and drove 175 miles to her home in Melvern, Kansas. The FBI has investigated hundreds of kidnapping cases over the years, but few, if any, were as gruesome and ghastly as the kidnapping of a fetus.

The FBI would have assisted state and local police agencies in the investigation of the Skidmore case whether or not a federal crime had been committed. What made this particular kidnapping a federal crime, or "FBI matter", as

Larry King put it, was that the kidnapped fetus was taken across state lines, from the place of the kidnapping in Missouri to the home of Lisa Montgomery in Kansas.

Of course, the fetus I have been referring to was no longer a fetus after the crime; it was a newborn baby. Miraculously, the baby survived the ordeal and was recovered and returned to Bobbie Jo's husband after the arrest of Montgomery. After these events, my job was to communicate what happened, the status of the investigation at the time and what might transpire going forward.

For many law enforcement officers, after years of getting a up close and personal view of the terrible things that human beings do to one another, there is a tendency to compartmentalize emotions so they don't affect other aspects of their lives. This is why a law enforcement officer, teaching a citizens' academy about homicide investigations, for example, can show grisly crime scene photos in a nonchalant and routine manner, while the business people and retirees in the audience become revolted enough to leave the room. The citizens have not learned the fine art of compartmentalizing their emotions. Law enforcement officers do this instinctively. Otherwise, it would be impossible to be an effective investigator.

On the other hand, for my television interview with Larry King, I was not in the role of an investigator. I was a communicator. My instincts told me that in this role, a genuine expression of empathy was not only appropriate, but a necessary and effective way to communicate.

The circumstances of this case went far beyond the hundreds of violent crimes that law enforcement agencies investigate every day in the United States. This murder was truly a crisis for the family and, moreover, the community as a whole. To be sure, every crime victim experiences a crisis of his or her own. But the nature of this crime, the fact that it occurred in a town covering less than one-third of a square mile with a population under four hundred and the enormous media attention it brought to bear made this a community crisis event.

When a person speaks to the public, whether it is face-to-face or through a medium like television, it is important that there is a message in the communication. In this case, the message can be simply that law enforcement is on the job, working the investigation to make sure that the person responsible is brought to justice. That can be conveyed by a person being present on television and answering the questions posed to them by the interviewer ("Is this an FBI matter?").

In a crisis, there needs to be more. People affected by the crisis want and need to know that you care about them and the effect the crisis has had on their lives. This is absolutely imperative if you or your organization caused the crisis to occur, but it is still necessary even when that is not the case, because you are still going to be involved with the solution and in helping return their lives to any possible sense of normalcy.

In this case, my message was very simple: We cared about the effect the crisis had on the family of Bobbie Jo and others.

Showing that you care will go a long way towards returning things to normal in the aftermath of a crisis. It will gain you the trust of your audience. This is exactly what Rudy Giuliani did during the crisis caused by the attacks of September 11, 2001. Giuliani made communication his priority in helping the residents of New York City recover from the crisis. His genuine statements of empathy helped establish his leadership and gain him the trust of a deeply wounded city and country.

So, how does one convey to the public that the FBI and its law enforcement partners care deeply about the people who are affected by this terrible tragedy? It is accomplished by talking from the heart and demonstrating empathy to Bobbie Jo's immediate family and others.

There was however, the little matter of Larry King's question to me: "Agent Lanza, is this an FBI matter?"

So I answered the question, but then got to the most important message: "Yes it is Larry, but I would first like to say that our hearts go out to the family of Bobbie Jo and those affected by this terrible tragedy."

It took just four seconds to deliver a message of empathy, show people that we cared and that we were more than just law enforcement officers compartmentalizing our emotions to investigate a crime. We cared about the victim, the victim's family and the entire community affected by the crisis and we were there ultimately to help make things better.

What I did on Larry King Live was nothing extraordinary. All I did was respond during a crisis by telling people my true feelings about their situation. So often this is forgotten by business leaders and communicators who are trying desperately to gain the trust of those affected by a crisis.

Recent news provides two high-profile examples of corporations which experienced a crisis and did not immediately show empathy to the people affected by the crisis. Toyota Corporation's response to a crisis affecting thousands of automobile owners helped to tarnish their reputation because they waited too long even to admit there were problems with their accelerators in some cars.

The response of BP to the crisis affecting millions of people, not to mention the families of the eleven who died when an offshore oil rig exploded and began spewing thousands of barrels of oil into the Gulf of Mexico, was an exercise in the blame game.

Both of these companies lost credibility and trust simply because they did not quickly acknowledge either the crisis they caused or, even more importantly, that they cared about the people affected. They lost trust right at the starting gate, and their reputations and value to customers may be forever diminished.

Larry King provided me the opportunity to express empathy for the crisis I was talking about. The real extraordinary work came not from me, but from the investigators who solved the case and returned Bobbie Jo's baby to her father.

It was the tenacious work of law enforcement officers from the Missouri Highway Patrol and the FBI which led to the determination that chat messages received by Bobbi Jo, which were still present on her computer at the time of her murder, originated from the home of Lisa Montgomery. Her arrest and the recovery of the baby came shortly thereafter. It was law enforcement and high-tech detective work at its best.

All I did was talk about it on Larry King Live because it was, after all, "an FBI matter."

Chapter 7

Connie Chung's Terrible Show

Working with the media as an FBI spokesman can be an arduous job and it is certainly one that requires a great deal of patience, but for me it was a labor of love. When I applied for the position as spokesperson, I didn't think I would have that responsibility for very long - two or three years at the most. Each time the media called, it was a challenge for me to find a way to meet their needs and at the same time not violate FBI policy by releasing certain sensitive information. I found this to be mentally stimulating and, overall, a very positive experience. The fundamental key to meeting this challenge and being a successful spokesperson involved building relationships with the media. I tried to do this with the local media by visiting the television and radio stations and meeting with reporters just to shoot the breeze. I would go there at times when they were not under pressure to meet a story deadline.

On these occasions I became acquainted with reporters, editors and producers, and began to see that most of them were very intelligent and decent people who did not have an agenda or a bias against the FBI. They weren't planning tricks to get information or trying to make people look deceitful or dimwitted on television. Most went into broadcast or print journalism because they wanted to provide a public service, to communicate information in an objective way.

Most of the reporters I worked with over the years I liked. There were some exceptions, but even in these cases it wasn't personal. Often, the acts of the reporter were not driven by personality so much as by the demanding forces of the fiercely competitive 24-hour news business.

In December, 2004, worldwide media attention focused on the small town of Skidmore, Missouri following the murder of Bobbie Jo Stinnett and kidnapping her unborn fetus. Prior to discussing this case with the media, I advised them of certain things that I could not address, such as specific evidence the FBI had gathered or theories on the motivation for the crime. Some reporters choose to disregard the ground rules I had set for the topics of discussion and asked me questions about those areas on live television. This is not common, but it is most likely to occur in crisis situations when you are communicating with reporters with whom you have no previous working relationship. The best way to handle situations like that is to tell the reporter that you cannot answer the question and provide some information that you can talk about. It is unwise to make an issue of the question or to bring to the reporter's attention that they are violating the ground rules you set. If you do this, you will appear to the viewing public as evasive, since you they have not been privy to your pre-interview conversations with the media.

This happened in three consecutive interviews I did with the media in the aftermath of the Stinnett murder. I was expecting it to occur again during an interview I was doing on the *Today Show*, with its host Campbell Brown. I had told the producer of the *Today Show* the topics I couldn't discuss during the interview. Given the climate of news reporting focusing on the horrible details of the tragic murder, I was prepared for the same from the *Today Show*. In stark contrast to previous interviews, Brown not only showed sensitivity to issues I couldn't talk about in the case, she took the story in a positive direction by focusing the elation agents felt when they found the baby alive.

In this type of climate, or any for that matter, a television station has to do one thing above all else - make a profit. I don't take exception to the notion that news is a profit-driven business. The station's owners invest in the infrastructure to bring us the news and they deserve to be financially rewarded for their investment. What is troublesome to me is how the news is sometimes promoted to achieve that end. One example is the overuse of superlatives (worst, best, longest, most heinous, latest, first time ever, etc.) to describe news stories. This unsettles me because in many cases such labels are merely given to attract attention to the story for promotional purposes.

Of greater concern is when reporters or producers embellish the facts surrounding a story. Sometimes this is done as they are introducing a story and setting up the facts for the audience immediately before they interview people to discuss the situation. Most interviewees let the embellishments go by without challenge, possibly because they are too focused on how they are going to answer the reporter's questions and don't catch it, or they assume it is not their place to challenge a news reporter or an anchor's statements. I believe that it is the responsibility of spokespersons not only to provide accurate facts to the public, but also to correct any misinformation that may exist or has been presented about a situation.

Once I was being interviewed with another person who decided to challenge a statement that had been made by the host. I believe this may have led to a very prominent journalist losing her job at CNN. It was the day of Connie Chung's terrible show.

Connie Chung started her career with a great deal of journalistic integrity. And she nailed some pretty high profile interviews, including one with U.S. Representative

Garry Condit after Sandra Levy's disappearance and the first interview of basketball star "Magic" Johnson following his public acknowledgement that he was HIV positive. Later, though, she trended toward tabloid stories which I think detracted from the respect she had attained reporting impartially on important news.

One particular Chung interview exemplified the degraded level of the style and substance of her journalism. It happened in 1995, when Chung was the host of *Eye to Eye*, a news magazine program that was being broadcast by the CBS network. During one segment, she was interviewing Kathleen Gingrich, the mother of Newt Gingrich, the Republican Speaker of the House. During the taping of the interview, Chung asked Ms. Gingrich what her son thought of First Lady Hillary Clinton. Ms. Gingrich refused to answer the question on the air. Chung then asked her to "just whisper it to me, just between you and me." Based on the way the question was posed, I would have assumed the same thing that Ms. Gingrich did, that the statement was off the record. Ms. Gingrich replied that she thought of the First Lady as a "bitch." Chung chose to broadcast the comment when the interview was aired.

That did it for me. I was not a big fan of Chung's style at this point in her career, but after the "whisper in my ear" trick, you could count me as a definite detractor.

Several years later, Chung was hosting a CNN prime time news program, *Connie Chung Tonight.* A producer with the show phoned me to request an interview. He had been watching the newswires and came across a story in which I was quoted. The situation involved a police investigation into racially demeaning letters that had been mailed by an unknown suspect to several African-American-owned businesses and churches in the Kansas City area. The mailings occurred around the anniversary of Martin Luther King's birthday, and although they did not contain any direct threats, the letters were racially charged, containing comments such as, "Aren't you glad Martin Luther King is dead?" It was clear that the letters were most likely sent by a very disturbed person with deep-rooted bigotry.

Since there were no threats in the letters, there was no violation of federal law. When this is the case, the FBI usually does not get involved in an investigation, but often offers assistance to local police agencies. Since similar letters had been sent two years prior to this occasion, the Kansas City, Missouri Police Department asked for help from one of our agents who specialized in hate crimes. It was thought that a coordinated effort and sharing of information might lead to the identification of the perpetrator, who could then be prosecuted by county officials for harassment.

The Kansas City Star had reported the incident and the Associated Press was in the process of doing a follow-up story. After the police mentioned that the FBI was involved in the investigation, I received a phone call from the AP reporter who quoted me in her story. My quote was subsequently seen by the CNN producer.

The producer asked if I would be willing to go on *Connie Chung Tonight* to be interviewed by Chung about the letters. He told me that a minister from one of the churches which received a hate letter had agreed to go on the show and they needed the law enforcement perspective to complement the minister's interview.

I was very surprised that this situation was rising to the level of national news, so I made it clear to the producer that the FBI was merely assisting in the case and at that point, no federal crime had even been committed. I did this for two reasons. First, I wanted him to be clear on the facts before he decided to plan for his evening show. Secondly, I wanted to make sure he didn't make the letters sound more grave and threatening than they were. Granted, it was a serious incident of bigotry, but it was not widespread and none of the involved parties - the FBI, the police or the recipients of the letters - believed that anyone was in danger.

In my experience with the media, the fact that the FBI is involved in an investigation heightens their interest in a matter because they know that the Bureau, for the most part, only investigates serious crimes. The media don't really care why the FBI is involved, only that they are, because they believe it will create and keep viewer interest in the news segment.

I am not saying that cases which the police investigate without the FBI are not serious. However, this case was not the type of story that is usually on national news programs. The fact of the FBI's involvement was used to make the incidents seem more severe. The CNN producer's fundamental job was to draw eyeballs to *Connie Chung Tonight*. It didn't really matter how he got them, just that they were there. FBI involvement in the case was the key to making the story part of their prime time news. I am not sure they would have broadcast the segment about the letters if I had not agreed to go on the show.

So, with a prime time slot in mind, the producer really did not care to hear my explanation that it was not a federal crime and that the FBI was only assisting the police department. All he really knew and cared to know was that this was a racially charged incident and that the FBI thought it was serious enough to get involved. That, in a television producer's mind, made it good enough to be the substance of a compelling news story. If it wasn't compelling enough, they could make it seem that way, which is exactly what they tried to do.

I made my way over to the Time Warner studio in Kansas City to be interviewed remotely by Connie Chung. I was anticipating a very benign segment, with the minister talking about the letter he received and me talking about what the police and FBI were doing about it. What I didn't anticipate was that Connie Chung could have been fired from her two-million-dollar-a- year job as a result of the interview.

I met the minister at the studio and had a few minutes to talk to him about the hate letter his church had received. In preparation for our joint interview, the minister and I were seated next to one another in the Kansas City studio while Chung sat at the anchor desk in New York. Each of us had an internal feedback device[1] placed in our right ears and a small microphone clipped to each of our ties.

After we were all wired up, a director in New York spoke to each of us to make sure we could hear the studio in New York. He asked us to count to ten to make sure our

[1] The internal feedback device, known as an IFB in the broadcast business, is a tiny headphone that fits into your ear. It is connected to a flesh colored wire that runs up over your ear and connects to another coiled wire and eventually to the wireless receiver which is tuned to the studio sound, in this case coming from New York. If the IFB is placed on you correctly and fits your ear properly, it is imperceptible to the television audience. If not, the audience can see the coil attached to your collar, which makes it look like you are plugged into an electrical outlet. Worse, the earpiece may protrude in a way that looks like a giant ball of wax is falling out of your ear. I did these remote interviews so often that I actually had a custom- fitted ear piece made especially to fit the crevices and contours of my ear. It was not very expensive and I would recommend the investment to anyone who might be doing a lot of remote interviews. It works like a champ and you don't have to stick something in your ear that is used by dozens of other people.

microphones worked properly. He told us that Chung would introduce the segment about the hate letters and that she would ask the minister a couple of questions first and then do the same with me. We were told that the interview with both of us would last about four minutes.

As far as live television interviews go, this one was not particularly nerve-wracking for me. The facts were very straightforward, and since we were looking for a suspect I had a lot more leeway in what I could say, because the publicity served a law enforcement function. Media publicity often results in information being provided by the public which helps solve a case, so FBI policy allowed me to release a lot of information about the crime. I wasn't overly worried about saying something I wasn't allowed to say, which is often a concern during media interviews.

As the interview was about to begin, our audio connection went live, and through our IFBs, we could hear what Chung was saying to the television audience. Both of us listened intently as Chung introduced the segment by adding some embellishment to the story. "Racial tensions are at an all-time high in Kansas City..." As Chung spoke those words, I saw the minister let out a sigh and glance over to me as if to indicate his total disapproval of the way the story was being couched. Chung's introduction of the segment lasted about 20 seconds, during which I could sense the minister's increasing agitation in the way his upper body stiffened. The more Chung spoke, the stiffer he got. At that moment I knew that this interview was not going to start out in a good way for Connie Chung.

After the introduction, Chung asked the minister a question. He was clearly not happy with the way the story had been represented and wanted to clarify the situation for the public. He calmly told her to wait a minute, and that he had heard what she said in introducing the segment. He further explained that racial tensions were not at an all-time high in Kansas City, and that we had not had *any* racial tension in Kansas City since the 1960s.

Chung paused. I remember a couple of seconds of silence, which is an *eternity* in live television. Clearly uncomfortable, Chung searched for a reply. Finally she just said, "Oh." This was followed by more dead air while Chung regained her footing. She mentally regrouped and directed a question to me, asking about the status of the federal investigation into the mailing of threats. I felt bad for doing it, but I had to tell her that there were no threats mailed and therefore no federal crime and no formal investigation, only assistance on our part. I had to be honest. Chung responded with *more* dead air - about two seconds, to be exact. This was on top of the other dead time we had already experienced following the minister's correction. The interview was going down the tubes, in a slow and excruciating way.

Chung recovered enough to ask a few more questions of each of us, but since they were based on embellishment and the false pretense of race riots in Kansas City, they seemed quite inane. The damage was done. I tried to help her out with a message about the letter representing racial hatred in its purest form, but it was really too late to make the interview compelling television. All in all, Chung's interview of us was simply terrible.

The minister and I walked out of the studio together, just shaking our heads at the way the story had been characterized. I told him that he had a lot of guts to challenge Chung on live television and we both agreed that it was necessary to set the record straight.

What is important to remember about the tendency of journalists to embellish stories or even add "facts" that don't exist is that the person being interviewed should always take the opportunity to correct the misinformation. Otherwise, the viewing public may accept the false information and believe erroneously that there are race riots in the streets or, for that matter, any other embellishment. The minister's effort to correct Chung was a smart idea and one that should be kept in mind if the press tries to blow things out of proportion.

Several weeks later, I was reading the newspaper and saw a story indicating that *Connie Chung Tonight* had been discontinued by CNN. This was not a big surprise given that critics had already panned the show. What was a surprise, however, was the quote from the boss of Time Warner (the parent company of CNN), Ted Turner. He was quoted in the newspaper story as saying that *Connie Chung Tonight* was "just terrible." I really had to laugh at that one because I believe, given this quote, that Turner was watching Chung's interview with the minister and me. Maybe he based his opinion on our interview with Chung. If that was the case, it is possible that we were responsible for getting Chung's show canned by CNN. I don't really think that was the main factor, but given the type of journalist Chung had become, I like to think it did play a role.

Chapter 8

Noise Reduction

One of my most memorable national interviews was on the ABC network program *Good Morning America*. I was being interviewed live on the program in Kansas City by their host from New York. The interview had been scheduled the night before, so I knew exactly what time I was going to be on the air. This allowed me to give my parents, who live in Connecticut, a heads-up to tune in. After my appearance on the show, I spoke to my mother on the phone. "How do you think the interview went?" I asked her.

After I asked this question, there were about three seconds of silence, which I have found is never a good sign when you are looking for an opinion. This case was no exception to the rule. "Well, you were blinking a lot. Were the lights real bright in there? Because you were blinking quite a bit," my mom said.

"I didn't realize that, Mom. I didn't think the lights were that bright. I wasn't aware of any excessive blinking on my part," I responded.

"Oh, I went to see my hairdresser today. She watched it too," my mom said.

"Really?"

"Yes, she thought your mustache was too bushy."

"Thanks for letting me know."

I certainly learned one thing from that conversation with my mother about my appearance on *Good Morning America*: this is why children move away from home. I do not mean to suggest that I do not care for my parents. Truly, they have been extremely supportive of me throughout my life, for which I am very appreciative. And, in all seriousness, the observations of my mother and her hairdresser provided me with valuable information. Their comments reinforced the notion that visual distractions, or "silent noise," can detract from your intended message. For this reason, it is your responsibility as a communicator to eliminate as many of these distractions as possible in order to deliver a message without interference.

There are several things to think about when you want to eliminate distractions.

Clothing: When you are getting ready to appear on the public stage, whether in person or on television, your wardrobe is one of the easiest things you can control. Your clothing says a lot about you, and if not chosen carefully, it can be a major distraction. Be mindful that, as a communicator, your primary goal is to deliver a message, no matter the topic or the audience. With this in mind, understand that you and your message are a product in the audience's eyes, and most products don't sell very well without good packaging.

For television appearances, it may help you to look at what people are wearing on network news programs and follow their example. Network anchors and reporters have lots of people who specialize in clothing and makeup to make them look their best. You can get a good idea of what looks good if you follow their lead. Here are some general rules of thumb for television interviews to avoid distractions and appear your best:

- Don't wear pinstripes, herringbone, checks, plaids, or anything with narrow lines. These create moiré, an interference pattern that sometimes forms when a clothing pattern comes into conflict with the television's scanning system. The effect makes it appear as though an article of clothing is moving on the screen. This applies to all clothing, including ties and accessories.

- In general, solid muted colors look best. Wild patterns can look even wilder on camera.
- Any clothing with excess ruffles should also be avoided because it may be a distraction.
- White shirts can create an exposure problem, especially with people who have darker complexions. Often the shirt will be overexposed, making it difficult to balance the brightness of the shirt with a dark suit or background. If the shirt is properly exposed, then your skin tone might be underexposed. A light blue or gray shirt may be a better selection. Black clothing can create the opposite problem, and if the background is dark it can seem to disappear.
- Often jewelry that looks good to the eye can be distracting on camera. Large flat surfaces can cause an interfering glare. Anything that jangles or dangles can not only be visually annoying, but can create problems with microphone audio. Don’t accessorize with anything that will draw attention away from your message.
- It is said that the camera adds fifteen pounds, so keep that in mind when dressing. If your outfit makes you look a little heavy in the mirror, it will be even worse on camera.
- It is wise to avoid hats. People most likely to wear a hat are sheriffs or highway patrol officers. If you must wear a hat, it will need to be tilted back on your head so your eyes don't disappear in the shadows created by the brim.
- Women should avoid low-cut blouses for obvious reasons. If you are wearing a jacket for a sit-down

interview, pull the jacket down from the back and sit on the tail. It will help keep it from bunching around your shoulders and neck and giving a hunchback effect. Also, keep your jacket buttoned for a neater look.

- Make sure your tie and accessories are adjusted and in place before starting the interview. Don't hesitate to ask the interviewer if everything looks okay before starting the interview.

Background: I first realized the importance of a good background for television early in my career, when I watched one of my taped television interviews. During the segment, I couldn't help but observe how gigantic my head appeared on the television screen. Anyone else who saw the segment surely would have detected the same thing and have been distracted by my head's enormity. They probably hadn't remembered (or even heard) anything I said. As with clothing, anything unusual or out of the ordinary in your surroundings or personal appearance tends to become the focus of your audience, which diverts their attention from your spoken message. This is especially true when the viewing audience might be watching on a widescreen television, which makes images appear even larger.

When I saw the interview with my oversized head, I decided I did not want to continue as a spokesman unless I could find a way to avoid appearing on television as though I was a float in the Macy's Thanksgiving Day Parade. As it turned out, the solution was very simple. I started using a background prop.

The prop I used was the FBI seal, which appeared beautifully on camera. I placed the seal strategically behind me on the wall where I conducted most of my television interviews. I placed a tiny nail in the wall and hung the seal so that it would appear just over my shoulder on television. The FBI seal contained the name of my employer and its parent agency, the Department of Justice. It also included the FBI motto, "Fidelity, Integrity and Bravery," and the symbolic scales of justice, all on a nice backdrop of red, blue and gold colors. The seal identified who I represented, imparted an impression of authority to the interview, and just plain looked nice in the picture. For these reasons, the photographers videotaping my interviews always widened the shot to include the seal. This made my head size appear more normal, or, at least, less gigantic. Not having the distraction of an unusually large head to gawk at, viewers were more apt to listen to what I said and pay attention to my message.

As a spokesman, you should always use some type of background prop. If you are speaking on behalf of an organization, your company seal makes a good prop. Ideally, you should have something that relates to the news story you are talking about. For example, if you are talking about the Internet, a computer makes a great prop. If you are talking about the importance of family in bringing up moral children, a family picture is a good background prop. Other potential background props for television include a flag, a painting, a lamp, a bookcase or a plant. A blank wall or space behind you should be avoided. When you don't have a background prop, the photographer has only you to videotape, and this could potentially lead to the unflattering "giant head effect," detracting from your message.

The methods I have described apply to outdoor interviews as well. For these interviews, you should still include background props as much as possible. A sign with your company's name on it works very well, as does a flowering garden or a city scene. The photographer will usually help with this but he or she is generally more concerned with lighting then with the background.

If possible, when you are doing an interview outside, have another person with you who can help keep the area clear of distractions. Former vice presidential candidate Sarah Palin once had a memorable problem with a background that contradicted her message. She was being interviewed live on the *Today Show* from a farm around the time of the Thanksgiving holiday. Mrs. Palin was describing how her family was not going to eat the traditional turkey dinner on Thanksgiving that year because they wanted to spare a turkey's life. Directly behind her during the interview, there was a gentleman slaughtering turkeys, chopping their heads off in full view of the television audience. Unless her message was that someone from her staff should be fired, I am sure you agree that this background detracted from her intended message.

Another example of how important it is to keep your background secure from things that may detract from your message occurred in Albuquerque, New Mexico, where an FBI spokesman was doing a live television interview. As the interview was taking place and being broadcast to the city, a woman in the background stood up, removed all of her clothing, folded it in a neat pile, took a quick dip in a water fountain and started running up behind the FBI agent in full camera view. As she closed the distance from the fountain to the agent, neither the reporter nor the FBI agent had any idea what was going on behind them or that their newscast was quickly becoming R-rated. Fortunately, the photographer ran an interception pattern from behind his camera around the reporter and agent and stopped the woman about twenty feet from the camera. I cringe thinking about what would have happened had the photographer not placed his camera on a tripod. If he had been shooting the interview with his camera perched on his shoulder, he would not have been able to interrupt the live broadcast to stop her and there was no one else there to make the crucial cutoff.

Being interviewed on television outside can be hazardous to your message. I doubt many people watching that interview even knew what the agent was talking about. To control the background during outdoor interviews, it is wise to have as little space as possible behind you and have someone with you to help manage unanticipated situations.

While on the topic of background distractions, I want to mention the tendency people have to stand awkwardly behind another speaker. I have taken part in many press conferences over the years, and the staging of people in front of an audience was nearly identical each time. The main speaker was always standing behind a podium, and other people, awaiting their turn at the microphone or to be publicly recognized, would stand in a straight line behind the speaker. Most of time, these people didn't seem to know what to do with their hands. These useful extremities made a magical transition to awkward appendages when their owners were in front of an audience. Most people crossed their hands in front of them as if to protect their private parts from exposure. If I remember correctly, in not one of these press conferences were the people naked. Therefore, there was no reason to stand in the fig leaf position. When you are standing in front of an audience, the best place to put your hands is by your side. You may feel uncomfortable doing this, but force yourself. It looks much better. Both men and women should keep their hands by their sides.

Makeup: On September 26, 1960, as seventy million people watched, John Kennedy and Richard Nixon engaged in the first televised debate between two presidential candidates. Kennedy seemed to already know the power of the visual component of effective message delivery. He used makeup to reduce facial shine and the appearance of any imperfections that could compromise his message. He appeared tanned and well-rested, as if he had just gotten off a boat in Hyannis.

Nixon, on the other hand, appeared less easy on the eyes. He had a five o'clock shadow, was visibly perspiring, and appeared somewhat gaunt from his bout with a recent knee infection and a cold.

Following the first debate between the two candidates, a poll to determine the winner was conducted by a Philadelphia-based market research firm. The poll found a large discrepancy between the people who had watched on television and those who had listened to the debate on the radio. The poll showed Nixon winning among radio listeners 43 percent to 20 percent, and Kennedy winning among TV watchers, 28 percent to 19 percent. The poll was not done scientifically, so the results did not meet acceptable scientific standards for validity and therefore do not allow us to draw empirically based conclusions or generalizations. With that being said, I still believe, based on my own personal experience, that visual distractions can, without a doubt, detract from a communicator's message.

It is evident that my excessive blinking and bushy mustache impeded the communication of my message to my mother and her hairdresser. If you had asked my mom what I said during the interview on *Good Morning America*, she might have been at a loss. But she probably could have told you my exact BPM (blink rate per minute), plus or minus 5 percent. My mom's hairdresser, on the other hand, was probably thinking of how she might apply her thinning shears to my mustache, not how I responded to the queries of the news reporter.

These are not the only comments I have heard about my various television appearances which provided me with ample evidence of viewer distractions. For example, I have been told by various acquaintances over the years some of the following things:

"Your hair looked really gray." (It is now; it wasn't then).

"You looked like you hadn't slept all night."

"You had big bags under your eyes."

"Your nose looked out of proportion to the rest of your face." (That one hurt.)

"Your face looked a little bit shiny."

The commentary wasn't all bad. After seeing me interviewed on television, one person said, "You looked like George Clooney," but quickly added, "It was the way your hair was blowing in the wind. You don't really look like George Clooney."

People's perceptions of a person based on a television image can vary widely. When I have run into people that have seen me on television, there has been more than one instance when have been told that I was shorter in person than the viewer imagined I would be. I heard a few times that I looked younger in-person than on TV. On one occasion a woman said to me, "You must be proud to have your son follow you in your line of business."

"What do you mean?" I asked.

"Your son is an FBI agent, isn't he?" she said.

"My son is in high school," I told her.

"Then who is that person with your last name that I see on TV talking about the FBI?" she asked.

"That's me," I said, while trying to figure out whether I looked really young on TV, really old in person, or both.

I realized, of course, that I wasn't on television as part of a beauty pageant. It was all about delivering a message effectively. But the comment about the shine in particular got me thinking that there was at least one thing I could control. Professional news anchors, men included, use powder to reduce shine. Why not me? So one day I decided to pick up a powder compact for just that purpose. It was perfect, because it was small and easily hidden in my pocket, so I could keep it out of sight and didn't have to carry around a makeup bag. It included everything I needed: the powder, which matched my skin tone (chosen with the help of my wife); a blotter for the oily areas of my face; and a small mirror to make sure that I had not applied it too liberally or left any streaks. I made sure I had the compact with me whenever I was going to be interviewed on television.

One day I did a series of interviews on various network shows including the *Today Show* and *Fox News*. Each time, before I had a chance to pull out my compact and apply some powder, the television photographer grabbed his own make-up brush and delicately applied a thin coating of powder to shiny spots on my forehead and nose. As the photographers worked, they were able to see the results of their efforts in real time by looking at my image on the television monitor. This allowed them to apply powder with just the right touch for a natural look without reaching cakey-looking overkill. They were professionals. In each of these cases, I left the makeup job to someone who clearly knew what they were doing.

The last interview on that particular day was with Wolf Blitzer, the highly paid prize property and centerpiece of CNN's evening program lineup. Blitzer, by the way, was not a man who suffered from male-patterned baldness. He had a pronounced mane of silver gray hair with a beard to match. I wondered if he was called Wolf because it was short for Wolfgang or because his hairy head and face bore a striking resemblance to the animal.

In any case, I was getting ready to be interviewed on live national television by Blitzer. The interview was going to take place at the television studio of the Kansas City PBS affiliate. Having arrived early, I had plenty of time to prepare for the questions and to make sure that I looked presentable. I had been interviewed many times that day on the same issue, so communicating the information and my message was not going to be a problem. I used the extra time to make sure I looked my best and to eliminate any distractions in my appearance.

I was escorted into the studio by one of the video technicians and seated in a chair on the set where the interview with Blitzer was going to take place. It was late in the day, and by this time the previous applications of powder had lost their ability to counteract the emerging shine across my forehead and dark circles under my eyes. As I was being outfitted with a microphone and earpiece by the technician, I asked if he could apply some powder to my face. I had thought about using my own compact to do this myself, but prior to my other interviews that day, the professionals had provided the makeup application, with good results. I figured, why not go that route again? I was not an expert in this area. Unbeknownst to me, this guy wasn't either.

"Can you put a little powder on my face?" I asked.

"Powder?" he said, with a quizzical expression on his face. "I think we have some powder here. I will have to look."

At this point I should have realized that putting powder on a television guest's face was not something he normally did. I should have told him to forget it. But I had already made the request and I would have felt very awkward saying, "Oh, never mind."

He walked into another room, from which I heard the sounds of him rummaging around for makeup. The loud sounds of cabinet doors being opened and slammed shut and squeaky drawers being yanked back and forth on their rails emanated from his direction.

A few minutes later, he emerged from the room and approached me with a large tin can resembling the type of container my grandmother used to transport cookies to our house on holidays – only this one was three times as big. "Got some powder," he said gleefully.

Standing next to me, he opened up the can to display what I can only describe as a cache of face powder. There was so much of it that somehow it had settled into large mounds within the can, creating mini-mountains of makeup. I wondered why they had that much makeup at a PBS studio. Was Tammy Faye Baker coming there for an interview?

The mountains of makeup were almost picturesque, like a pristine painting suitable for a postcard, except for one thing: there was a small piece of wood sticking out of one the makeup mountains. I tried to think of a reason why there might be a random piece of wood in the makeup mountain until the technician reached his hand into the powder and yanked out the wooden thing, which, as it turned out, was part of a paintbrush. I deduced that the paintbrush, which, as far as I knew, was normally used for the application of many things other than makeup, was going to be used on my face.

What happened next occurred so quickly that I really didn't have time to stop it. He dipped the brush into the makeup and, without so much as shaking off the excess powder, began brushing long strokes up and down my face as if he were painting the side of a barn. Meanwhile, from the CNN studio in Atlanta, a voice directed at me said, "Agent Lanza, can you hear me?"

I hesitated to answer, fearful of getting my tongue coated in powder. I mumbled, "Yes."

The brushing continued as I heard the CNN voice say, "You are going to be on the air live with Wolf Blitzer in three minutes."

A few brush strokes later, the technician was finished. "There you go," he said.

As he picked up his can and walked away, I glanced down at my jacket pocket to dig out my compact, wanting to check its mirror to see if my face was presentable for television. I stopped short of pulling the compact of my pocket when I noticed my suit jacket. "Oh crap," I said, talking to no one in particular. My suit jacket was covered with a fine dusting of powder--shoulders, lapels, breast pocket, everything. I looked like I had been standing outside a Mary Kay factory at the time of a horrible explosion. I wondered, "If my suit looks this bad, my face must be…."

"Agent Lanza, you will be on in two minutes," the voice from Atlanta spoke again.

My compact mirror confirmed my worst fears. There were huge swaths and streaks of makeup all over my face. The powder had also somehow coagulated into tiny balls, which lodged themselves into my mustache. My eyelashes were somehow strong enough to support the weight of the powder as it clung to their ends. My eyebrows, formerly dark brown, were now a light shade of beige. That's when I realized why there was so much makeup on hand in the studio. It wasn't there for Tammy Faye Baker, it was there to make people *look* like Tammy Faye Baker. "You will be on in one minute," the voice said.

I had already brushed off my suit jacket, so I started working vigorously on my face, wiping and brushing off as much powder as possible in the little time that I had before the interview. Satisfied that I had removed the most noticeable excess, I looked down at my suit jacket. It was covered again! The powder had come off my face and landed on clothes. It wasn't as bad as before, but I still looked as if I had the world's worst case of dandruff. I was going to be talking to a national audience on Wolf Blitzer's show in a matter of seconds, so I brushed what I could off and straightened myself up for the interview. I made sure that when my mouth moved it didn't cause any visible cracks in the powder on my cheeks.

The interview began, and while I tried to stay focused as it progressed, I couldn't help but think that with the heavy dose of powder I may have looked as though I had been embalmed, which would have been a definite distraction from the delivery of my message.

As it turned out, there was no cause for worry after all. Watching the taped segment later, I could see no noticeable powder on my face or clothes.

From this episode, I learned a few important points about preparation which may help you in television interviews. For studio interviews, arrive at a television studio well in advance of the time you will be interviewed, and bring someone with you to help you get ready. Use the wait time to prepare for the interview mentally and to check your physical appearance. Try to eliminate anything that would cause a distraction for the viewer. Have a makeup compact with you to employ if the need arises. Don't ask anyone to apply makeup for you unless the person is a professional. How do you know if they are? If you have to ask them for makeup, they probably are not. Professionals will see the need and go to work to make you look good. Another clue to determine whether they know what they are doing: if they come at you with a paintbrush, they probably don't.

A final word on makeup: Recent advances in television technology have created challenges for people trying to maintain an attractive appearance on the tube. You might believe that more makeup would be required to optimize one's appearance on high-definition television, but according to experts, the opposite is true. Less is more. A different type of makeup, one that is silicone-based, is required for the best effect. Traditional powder sits on top of the skin and creates a coating. On high-definition television, this can be more noticeable. A silicone-based makeup is absorbed into the skin and looks more natural. Mostly, this is an issue for the pros, and not something to worry too much about for the occasional television interview. Your background and lighting, however, are things you can almost always control, and adjusting these two variables to the best extent that you can, will go a long way towards a good appearance that minimizes message noise.

Chapter 9

The Media Relationship

Communicators and journalists sometimes see each other in ways that can only be described metaphorically.

"The media are alligators," said an attorney that I know after he had a confrontation with the press. "If you are dealing with an alligator, you don't have to love the alligator. You don't even have to like the alligator. But you have to feed the alligator. If you don't feed the alligator, it will start feeding on rumor, innuendo and speculation," he further advised.

"They are the three monkeys," I heard one reporter say about communicators following a government press conference. "They've heard nothing, they've seen nothing and they SAY nothing!"

The respective metaphors express a sentiment that in each case is very likely born out of frustration. When it comes to professional journalists, it is far from the rule, but there are many cases when even respected professional media organizations have reported news based on information that was not verified for accuracy. The premature reports from *The New York Times*, *National Public Radio* and others that Congresswoman Gabrielle Giffords was dead after being shot in Tucson, Arizona are prime examples. As in most cases, these stories were quickly corrected, but the fact that it occurs frustrates communicators who endeavor to provide factual information, albeit not as quickly as the media would like.

From the media's perspective, communicators are sometimes seen as overly tight-lipped and secretive, creating frustration by thwarting the media from obtaining the information they need to report effectively not just breaking news, but the full depth and breadth of the story.

Invariably, there are going to be situations when the media is trying to obtain information that the communicator is trying to restrict. When this happens, a strong prior working relationship between the communicator and the media can go a long way towards all parties achieving their goals in adverse conditions.

Developing this working relationship hinges upon the communicator's ability to meet reporters and other media personnel and get to know them before a crisis occurs. If you establish yourself as a person who is credible, open, and willing to help the media, and as a person who doesn't try to hide information indiscriminately, you have taken the first step in achieving good media relations. A crisis is not the occasion to begin building relationships with the media. Relationships must exist before a crisis occurs.

During my eighteen years as an FBI spokesman, there were many situations when I had to withhold information from the media or ask them not to publicize information that they had. But there were always legitimate reasons for keeping the information under wraps. Sometimes these reasons were related to protecting the integrity of an investigation. Other times, it was an issue of federal privacy laws. In some cases, I withheld information to protect a victim's identity. Every so often, though, holding back information was a matter of life and death.

One such occurrence began at a very unique point in time: December 31, 1999, just hours before the end of the millennium. For many months leading up to the millennium, the FBI had been working on a national basis to prevent a terrorist attack, which some had speculated would take place at or near the beginning of the year 2000. To oversee the response and management of a terrorist incident anywhere in the country, a command post was established at the FBI headquarters in Washington, D.C.

The last day of the century had been very quiet across the country and it looked as if we were going to experience an uneventful evening in Kansas City. Many agents were relieved that the day had been peaceful, and they started to get ready to head home to celebrate New Year's Eve. This relief, however, was short lived. At about 5:00 p.m., I received a phone call from the FBI office in Kansas City. "Channel Nine is calling about the bank robbery. They would like you to call them back," our dispatcher said, in a nonchalant tone that indicated to me that he thought I had been notified already. His call was the first notice I received, so I told him I didn't know about the robbery and asked if he had any of the basic details.

"Just that the bank was robbed shortly before closing," he said, telling me the name and location of the bank.

As I started to phone the television station, I was thinking about the timing of the bank robbery, which took place a few minutes before closing time. At first, it seemed to me unreal that a bank robbery would occur during the last possible moments the bank could have been held up, not just for that day, but for that year, decade and century. However, upon further reflection, it seemed rather apropos that a bank robbery would occur at this significant time. In the early part of the twentieth century, the FBI's first major mandate was tracking down and arresting bank robbers.[2]

---

[2] In fact, the genesis of the modern FBI took place at Kansas City's very own Union Station, following a famous shootout with notorious bank robbers. The incident, known as the Kansas City Massacre, resulted in the deaths of four law enforcement officers, including an FBI agent named Raymond Caffrey.

Having spent untold hours investigating bank robberies in the twentieth century, it seemed only natural that we would end the century doing the exact same thing.

What I didn't realize at the time was that we wouldn't have to chase very far in this case, because this bank robber was still inside the bank, which had been surrounded by the police.

I contacted the television station as requested and spoke to their assignment editor, Tim Holderby, who is one of my favorite people in the news business. The assignment editor in a television news station is somewhat like the point guard on a basketball team. Just as the point guard directs a team towards the goal of scoring a basket, the assignment editor directs a news department towards the goal of creating a newscast. The assignment editor listens to the police and fire radio scanners, reads the newspapers, scans the Internet, and talks to the police, the FBI and other agencies, all in an effort to obtain the latest news of the day. If you have a story that you would like to broadcast on television news, the assignment editor is a good person to know.

Tim Holderby embraced his job with gusto and, at most times, a sense of humor. So when I asked him, "Isn't it wild that there would be a bank robbery at 5 o'clock on New Year's Eve?" I thought he was kidding when he said, "Yeah, and one with hostages!"

"No really, Tim, I will get you a description of the robber…" I started to say, brushing off his comment as a joke before he interrupted me.

"Really, there are hostages!" he said.

"I will call you back," I said.

"And the bank robber is a female!" he added.

I hung up the phone. A female robbing a bank is very unusual. Only about six percent of all bank robberies are carried out by females. Bank robberies that involve the taking of hostages are even less frequent, happening in less than one percent of all robberies.

I quickly dialed the FBI office and spoke to the dispatcher. "About that bank robbery," I said. "Is there something about the situation that you forgot to tell me?" There was silence on the other end of the phone.

"Are there hostages?" I prompted.

"That's what the police are saying," he said.

"Do you know if there have been any injuries?" I asked.

"Haven't heard." he replied.

A few minutes later, I was in my car, heading to the bank. On the way, I was provided with the details of what had occurred over the phone. A young woman, acting alone, had robbed the bank at gunpoint. A bank employee had triggered a silent alarm, to which the Olathe, Kansas police department had responded immediately. In fact, the police response was so immediate that they arrived at the bank just as the suspect was walking out the door. When the robber saw the police outside the front door, she retreated back into the bank, locked the front door and took six bank employees hostage.

The incident garnered a great deal of media attention, not only locally, but also on a national scale. The FBI and the media had been standing ready for the possibility of a terrorist event on New Year's Eve, and since this had not occurred, they turned their attention to the bank robbery. I learned later that Janet Reno, the United States Attorney General, and Louis Freeh, the Director of the FBI, sat next to one another in the FBI command post in Washington, D.C. with other law enforcement executives and watched our hostage situation in Olathe, Kansas unfold on the network news.

The Kansas City media covered the event with vigor, calling in reporters and photographers who had the evening off. These reporters and photographers came quickly to the staging area near the bank so they could report from their satellite trucks. One station summoned their traffic reporter and ordered him up in their airplane to report on the hostage situation from 3,000 feet above the bank.

The FBI and the police had contingents of SWAT officers surrounding the bank. Hoping to have a peaceful end to the situation, they waited patiently, but stood ready to take action if necessary. Near the bank, an FBI mobile command post was set up, which housed critical command personnel as well as several hostage negotiators.

For my part, I remained in the staging area in order to be as close as possible to the press. I briefed them on a regular basis, mainly to provide information to reporters arriving on the scene for the first time. There really wasn't much new to tell anyone, as the situation was in a holding pattern. SWAT members were holding off on any entry into the bank during this time because that would put the hostages in danger. The suspect wasn't giving up or coming out, thus creating the standstill. The task of resolving the standstill was given to the FBI hostage negotiators. However, the suspect refused to talk to them, despite their repeated attempts to reach her by phone inside the bank. Around 7:00 p.m., the stalemate was entering its third hour when the media figured out something that we didn't want them to report. Besides the hostages, there were several bank employees hiding in offices inside the bank. Someone with knowledge of this told the media and the reporters went to me for confirmation. The presence of the bank tellers was unknown to the bank robber, and I feared if the information were broadcast it would put the tellers in danger.

In any crisis situation, it is important to be cognizant that communications about the incident are reaching many different audiences, which in most cases is not a problem. But, in this scenario, it was possible that the bank robber was listening to news reports about the incident or talking to someone on the outside who was listening. Knowing that the suspect could potentially hear any of my comments that were broadcast was a little unnerving.

While the possibility of the suspect hearing my comments was certainly a concern of mine at this hostage situation in 1999, subsequent growth in communication technology has greatly increased the risk of accidentally communicating information to a criminal that is harmful to others. In a similar situation today, a smartphone in a suspect's hand would make it a virtual certainty they that could watch the news about their crime in real time.

Given the prospect that this bank robber was hearing what I said to reporters, I didn't want to talk about the people hiding in the bank, as it would obviously put them at great risk if the suspect learned that they were there. Moreover, I didn't want the reporters to broadcast even the slightest hint that there were others in the bank. In order to ensure this reporting didn't happen, I talked to the reporters on an off-the-record basis, explaining that we could only talk about information the suspect already knew, which was that she had six hostages, police and FBI were outside the bank and that we wanted her to talk to our negotiators to bring a peaceful resolution to the crisis. I explained that any further information would not be discussed by me and should not be broadcast at all. It was clearly an issue of safety that anyone could understand once the reasoning was explained.

In my experience, I have found reporters are much more willing to accept a communicator's unwillingness to talk about something if the reason is explained to them. Resorting to the stock phrase "no comment" when responding to questions that you are unwilling to answer usually causes a reporter to work even harder to get an answer to the question. I would like to state emphatically, without any reservation, that if you expect to communicate effectively, the words "no comment" should never cross your lips. Translated, "no comment" means "I know, but I am not telling you." (At least, that is what your audience may perceive). It is always better to explain the reason why you can't answer a question, so as not to leave the reporter wondering.

This is not to say that you should never withhold information if you have good reason to do so. Just don't withhold it by using that wording. If you do, your audience may perceive you as an antagonist, even if you haven't done anything wrong. At a minimum, using that phrase will make you seem secretive and mysterious, which is the exact opposite of how you want to be perceived if you expect to communicate effectively.

If you can't provide information, people want to know why. Explaining the reason is much better than giving an evasive and cagey "no comment," which will generally increase the communicator's level of discomfort by prompting more questions about the topic that they are unwilling to talk about.

During the bank hostage situation, an indiscriminate release of information could have resulted in safety issues for not only the hostages and others in the bank but also for the law enforcement officers on the scene. Even though the television photographers were restricted from getting close to the bank by a police-established perimeter, they shot images of the bank with zoom lenses. This allowed the viewing public to see live images of the police, FBI SWAT members and hostage rescue personnel in their positions outside the bank. Worse yet, one television station's traffic reporter was broadcasting video from an airplane above the bank, providing viewers with a bird's-eye view of the law enforcement operation.

I wasn't in a position to see what was being broadcast, but I was quickly alerted to the situation by the FBI command post. "Jeff, can you tell the media to get their plane out of there? They're showing video of our position at the bank. And they are also zooming in on us from outside the perimeter. They need to stop immediately."

"I'll take care of it," I replied, knowing that getting the media to remove the aircraft wouldn't require as much convincing as getting them to stop shooting video of the bank with their zoom lenses on the ground.

In the case of the aircraft, it only took one phone call by me to the news station which had their traffic reporter flying circles over the bank. "Can you remove the aircraft from the area? It's causing problems for our SWAT team. If the suspect is watching television, she will be able to see their exact position," I told the assignment editor.

"We'll do it, Jeff," he replied without question. He knew that if they were reluctant to comply voluntarily, there was an easy way to mandate the removal of the plane. Under these circumstances, the Federal Aviation Administration can establish a Temporary Flight Restriction in a certain area, which makes it unlawful for private pilots to intentionally cross into the area of restricted airspace. If an aircraft violates the order, military or law enforcement aircraft may be used to intercept it. In a case like this the pilot could risk losing their license to fly, effectively ending their career as an in-the-air traffic reporter.

"Thanks," I said, adding, "Can you also ask the photographers behind the perimeter to stop showing the position of our people at the bank?"

"I will let them know," he replied.

I followed that request with phone calls to the news departments of the other three television stations that were on the scene. Each person I spoke to had the same basic response as the first, which was that they were going to let the photographers know about my concern. What happened on the next several minutes I would describe as a minor brouhaha. I fielded an abundance of telephone calls from news directors. These calls concerned what their television stations were or were not shooting and their explanations why what they were doing wasn't wrong because they were only showing the front of the bank and not law enforcement personnel. In between phone calls, the reporters on the scene were receiving the same challenges to my request.

During this time, I also received phone calls from our command post, reiterating the problem with television images of the SWAT team at the bank, although they were not sure which television stations were the offending parties. Anxious to address the SWAT team's concerns about safety and to bring the confusion to a close, I said, "Look, if you are showing any images on television of FBI or police outside the bank, please stop. If the suspect has a television or is talking with someone who does, it puts everyone in danger." I was aware that the police could easily change the perimeter, which would have made it impossible for the television stations to obtain the video, but I preferred not to resort to forced movement. The stations were told in no uncertain terms the reason why we were telling them to do this, and they complied because they understood the risk.

The risk was based on the possibility that the suspect had access to a television and was watching it, and this possibility turned out to be a reality. She was watching news reports about her own bank robbery and hostage situation. She had real time information on what the news was reporting from outside of the bank, and this played a role in what transpired next.

One of the hostages, after watching part of the virtual non-stop coverage of the situation on a television in the bank, dialed Kansas City's ABC affiliate, KMBC-TV, on a cell phone and starting speaking with a reporter named Kris Ketz. As they were speaking, the suspect grabbed the phone from the hostage and spoke directly with the reporter. Part of the conversation was later broadcast:

Ketz: Why, I mean why do something like this?

Suspect: Because at first, yeah I was gonna rob this bank because I had nothing to lose. That's I what I told them, I told them my entire story, I had nothing to lose.

Ketz: What do you mean you had nothing to lose?

Suspect: I've lost it all. I mean, lost it all, lost my job, lost my family, lost it all.

The "them" the suspect was talking about were the hostages, to whom she had told her story. Besides her family and her job, the 23-year-old woman had lost all of her money at local casinos. Having "nothing to lose" was her reason for robbing the bank.

The suspect would not talk directly to our hostage negotiators, nor was she releasing all the hostages or coming out of the bank peacefully. She had let some hostages go, but six remained. While television reporter Kris Ketz talked to her on the phone, I received a phone call from the station's news director, Brian Bracco, who said, "Jeff, we have the suspect on the line. She is telling us she wants to talk to the FBI, but she doesn't know how to get in touch with them. Would you like to talk to her?"

Bracco and I had an excellent working relationship. In my early days as an FBI spokesman, I made it a point to meet all the news directors in Kansas City. It helps to know people that you might work with in advance of a crisis because it will make your later work under adverse circumstances go more smoothly. This situation definitely tested the boundaries and conflicts between the needs of law enforcement and the needs of the media.

The phone conversation the suspect had with Ketz was big news. It gave an insight into the motivation of the criminal in a live situation. This was a nationwide news story on a night when the media was ready for an event other than the ball dropping in Times Square. Channel Nine had an aspect of the story which nobody else did.

Law enforcement wanted the situation to end peacefully, and Bracco, based on our relationship, contacted me before making the decision about broadcasting the conversation between the suspect and Ketz. To obtain a peaceful ending to this situation, I knew it was of crucial importance for the suspect to talk to the negotiators. The FBI has specialists in every field office that receive weeks of special training to handle situations like this. They are experienced experts in the area of hostage negotiations and I was not. I did not want to talk to her, nor should I have been talking to her. I answered Bracco, "No, I am not the person. She really needs to be talking to the hostage negotiators. What is the number they can call?" I asked.

"She wants a number to call them, can you give it to me?" Bracco asked.

"I will call you right back with the number," I said. I quickly dialed the command post and asked for the number to the trailer where the hostage negotiators were stationed. I got the number and provided it to Bracco, who passed it along to the suspect.

What transpired next resembled something that might have involved the bumbling character, Chief Inspector Clouseau, in one of the Pink Panther movies.

A few minutes later, I got another call from Bracco. "Jeff, we just talked to the suspect again. She is calling the number you gave us for the negotiators and nobody is answering," he said.

"That can't be right, they are waiting for her call," I said. I double-checked that I had given him the right number. "I will call you back," I added.

I hung up the phone and called the number I had been provided for the negotiators. Someone answered on the first ring. "Hello," the agent said.

"This is Jeff Lanza. I was trying...,"

I was abruptly interrupted. "Jeff, you can't call on this number, it's reserved for us to talk to the suspect," barked the negotiator who answered the phone.

"I know, but she just tried to call you and you..." I figured it wasn't worth explaining. "She has your number and said she wants to talk to you," I said. "Can you stay by the phone?"

The suspect probably dialed the wrong number the first time when she got no answer. In any case, she eventually talked to the negotiators, but never agreed to give up. Shortly after 1:00 a.m. on January 1, 2000, one of the hostages knocked the gun out of her hand and it was retrieved by another hostage. The SWAT team quickly entered the bank and arrested the suspect with no shots fired. The incident was over more than eight hours after it had begun as a bungled bank robbery by a desperate young woman.

Ensuring public safety is the primary goal of any organization in a crisis situation. When the media arrives at a crisis event, though, their goal is to obtain the story. The lawyer I mentioned earlier may have likened the media to alligators with a constant appetite. But in my experience, with rare exceptions, most media professionals with whom I am familiar would never subjugate the need for public safety and security to the narrow demands of television ratings. However, conditions are not always so black and white. When there are gray areas, it is up to the communicator to help the media understand what is at stake and why. A terse "no comment" does not help. It fact, it usually makes matters worse.

Moreover, it is incumbent upon the communicator to build relationships with reporters, assignment editors, and managers of local media. An ongoing crisis situation is not the time to do this. Building relationships is problematic when you are being directed by your boss to get pictures taken off the television or when a reporter is being yelled at by his news director to get a scoop.

The time to develop relationships is before the crisis occurs. When it happens, the relationship that you previously built may pay dividends by helping you deliver your message in a way that allows both the communicator and the media to achieve their goals – and without either party being referred to as monkeys or alligators.

Chapter 10

The Control Factor

Success in the context of a communication with the media can be defined as achieving one's desired outcome by means of the provision of information to an audience. I have found that a very important element to this success is effective control, the level of which can be affected greatly by your actions as communicator. We have already covered steps a good communicator takes to control his or her own impact while imparting information, such as good preparation, speaking in sound bites and overall vigilance. However, there is another variable in the communication equation: the audience. Exerting the right sort of control over the receiver(s) of your communication can also be of crucial importance, especially if your communication will be filtered through the media. If you are involved in a crisis situation, controlling the audience variable is of the utmost importance. A good illustration of this is from my own experience with the media during kidnapping case of newborn baby named Carlie.

At 3:30 a.m. on January 29, 1998, I was awakened by the ringing of my phone. "Hello," I said, still shaking off my slumber.

"Jeff, this is Matt at the office. You need to go to KU Hospital," the voice on the other end said. He was referring to the University of Kansas Medical Center, a major research and patient care facility located in Kansas City, Kansas. "A newborn baby was kidnapped from the maternity ward."

"When?" I muttered.

"Late last night," he answered. "Taken right out of the mother's room." As I tried to wake up and think clearly, the gravity of the situation was sinking in very quickly. "The SAC wants you to get over to the hospital right away," he continued. He was referring to the Special Agent in Charge, the person who heads the FBI office in Kansas City.

The kidnapping of a child of "tender years" requires, per internal policy, that the FBI investigate immediately. A person of "tender years" is defined as anyone not having reached their eighteenth birthday. In this case, the kidnappee was truly of tender years – she was merely eight hours old at the time of the kidnapping.

As I drove over to the hospital, I thought about the kidnapping and wondered how anyone could possibly walk out of a hospital with a newborn baby that was not their own. Many kidnappings do not have happy endings, but the fact that the victim in this case was a newborn gave me a little encouragement. In cases of baby kidnappings, the motivation for the kidnapping is usually that the abductor couldn't have a baby and wants to raise the kidnapped baby as their own, not hold it for ransom. In ransom-seeking cases, it is much more likely that the kidnap victim will be harmed. In this case, however, it was a matter of following the evidence to those responsible and returning the baby to its parents.

As the spokesman for the FBI in Kansas City, my role in this investigation was to coordinate the publicity surrounding this event and to communicate information about the kidnapping to the media, who had already set up at the hospital by the time I arrived. Moving past them as I drove into the hospital parking lot, I was taken aback by the sheer number of reporters who had congregated at the early hour. At this juncture, the hospital was not providing any information to the media. Instead, they had relegated that task to the FBI. The only thing the media knew was that a kidnapping had occurred in the maternity ward of the hospital, which they had heard on police radio scanners. They didn't have any more details than that (as I learned from their numerous phone calls to me). They were hungry for news on the kidnapping, and they were starting to get a little antsy as their 5:00 a.m. news shows were getting closer to air time.

I knew that if I stopped my car anywhere near them, I would be surrounded as soon as I opened the door to exit the vehicle. With nothing to tell them at this point, I knew that was a bad idea. To set the stage for audience control, my first interaction with them in this situation would be an important one. I didn't want to be asked questions that I couldn't answer. Shrugging one's shoulders in response to basic questions is not a good way to begin a communication effort during a crisis. I had a feeling that this situation was going to be continuing for a while and I wanted to be in control from the very beginning, with tangible and factual information that I could tell them in a well-ordered fashion.

I parked my car away from the media on the east side of the hospital. As I exited my car I couldn't help but notice that I stood literally twenty feet from the border between Kansas and Missouri. The eastern side of the hospital is situated along State Line Road. On the hospital side of the road is the state of Kansas, but on the other side of the street is the state of Missouri. I knew that the proximity of the kidnapping to the state line could prove very important in terms of how the case would eventually be prosecuted. A kidnapping victim has to be taken across a state line for there to be federal jurisdiction. Federal prosecution of a case cannot take place unless this interstate transportation occurs. From an investigative standpoint, it really didn't matter. The FBI always investigates a kidnapping of a child, whether or not there is interstate transport of the victim, and in many cases, at least at the very beginning, the FBI has no way of knowing whether or not that has happened. If it turns out that there is no federal jurisdiction, those responsible are instead prosecuted by the state authorities where the kidnapping occurred.

I quickly walked into the hospital to receive a briefing by the agents working on the case. I was told the somber news that we had absolutely no information about the suspect or suspects in the kidnapping. After conducting interviews of all the possible witnesses, we knew not much more than when we started.

About all we knew at this point, was that at approximately 11:00 p.m., a suspect, identified as a woman, had walked into a hospital room where a mother and her newborn baby, named Carlie, were resting together following the birth. The mother did not remember much about the brief conversation she had with the suspect and fell asleep while the suspect was still in the room. When she awoke several minutes later, Carlie was gone.

All the people on staff on the maternity floor at the time of the kidnapping were interviewed. We learned from them that a man, apparently not visiting anyone in the hospital, had also been present for a short period on the maternity floor about the time Carlie was kidnapped. The witnesses could not provide good descriptions of either the man or the woman.

Before I went outside to talk to the media, the agent in charge of the investigation provided one more piece of evidence. "There is video surveillance from a basement security camera," he said. This got me excited, because I actually had something to give to the media, rather than just a verbal description of the suspects.

"What does it show?" I asked.

"Not much. There is a frame from the video that shows two figures walking out of the basement to a parking garage. It only shows their backs and it's very grainy. You can't tell much, although it looks like the man is holding a baby carrier," he informed me.

"Is there a time stamp?" I asked.

"Yes, around the time of the kidnapping," he replied.

"We should definitely release the picture to the media, even if there are no faces shown. It may lead to more information. Besides, anything is better than nothing at this point." I said.

A few minutes later he handed me the video and I proceeded outside to meet with the press. There was a chance, even without identifiable faces, that the video might prompt a member of the public to provide another lead. In any case, the media loves video, and at the very least it would give them something other than me to broadcast on the morning news.

Even though personnel from the hospital had not spoken to the media, they did set up a staging area for the press. This is extremely helpful in situations like this because the staging area is used to corral the media, in essence. The designated staging area was where all media briefings would take place. If the media wanted information about the kidnapping, they would have to remain in that area, which was at the corner of a parking lot on the hospital property. Having a staging area for the media is important in crisis situations because it keeps them physically controlled. It reduces the likelihood that they will add to the crisis by interfering with operations at an organization. If all official information is released from one location, it will deter the media from trying to obtain interviews in other locations and from people who may not have complete knowledge of the events, potentially creating misinformation and confusion about the crisis.

The establishment of a staging area in a crisis situation is important for yet another reason: to create an equal playing field for all media outlets. The media needs information for their news stories, and to maintain viewer interest in a developing story, they would prefer to have something new to report for every newscast. Additionally, each news media organization would like to have this information before their competition has it – for bragging rights, essentially. Being first to report a news development is a valued occurrence in a newsroom. Being last (or even second) to report a story, in the media's way of thinking, is an unmitigated disaster.

For this reason, the media is very concerned not only about getting information, but also about making sure that they are not missing any information that their competition may have. The establishment of a staging area, a place where all the media can get the same information at the same time, is of crucial importance, especially in a crisis. It creates not only physical control, but also psychological control, because nobody gets worried or upset that they might be missing out on news. The wrath of a reporter who gets beat to a big story or development can be severe, and it may disrupt the desired environment of calmness and order you have worked to maintain during a crisis. The establishment of a staging area will go a long way toward eliminating this possibility.

The KU Hospital staging area, since it was in a parking lot, was large enough to have room for reporters, photographers and satellite trucks from local media, as well as some that had arrived from nearby cities. The number of media people on site had grown in the time since I first drove past the staging area. Television reporters, numbering about half a dozen, were standing with microphones in their hands. Not far away from each reporter were photographers who had set up their camera tripods throughout the parking lot, as if to mark their territorial boundaries on the concrete. About ten other reporters from various radio and print media waited nearby.

With the surveillance videotape in hand, I walked across the driveway from the hospital to the staging area. The reporters, noticing my approach, left their position and walked towards me like a pack of hungry animals. Within a few seconds, I was surrounded. I use the term "hungry animals" in more than just a metaphorical sense. I don't mean this in a negative way, but the fact is, reporters feed on information – it is their livelihood in the news business. Having been deprived of information up to this point, they were very hungry for anything that they could use about the kidnapping for their upcoming newscasts. I was about to provide the feed.

Knowing that one of the most important factors in successful media communication is control, I stopped momentarily to speak to the reporters in order to tell them what to expect."I will provide some information about the kidnapping and then take a few minutes to try to answer your questions," I told them.

This type of opening statement is important for a communicator who is talking to the press. It tells the media what they can expect, and, in the process, sets an agenda for what is about to transpire. This is of practical value to the media, but it is even more useful to the communicator, because it establishes control. It tells the media who is in charge – in essence, it informs them that the communicator will be running the show when it comes to the dissemination of information. Having control from the outset is important because it tells the media that the communicator is there to help them, but that everybody has to play by the communicator's rules.

I provided the media with the basic information about the kidnapping, the limited descriptions of the suspects, and the grainy video of the backs of two people leaving the hospital about the time of the kidnapping. Then, I took a few minutes to answer their questions.

It is important that a communicator assert some element of control in the opening statement. I told the media at the outset that I would take a few minutes to answer their questions. This let them know that I was not going to stand there for a very long time. You might think that this would not be necessary because once the media is through asking questions, you are done. But, in my experience, they can always think of new questions to ask, or repeat the same basic questions phrased in a different way. There is nothing wrong with them doing this, as it is their job to gather information. Since they have to be there anyway, they might as well be trying to get more of it. So, unless a communicator wants to be talking to the media for an extended period of time, it is good practice to limit the question-taking period by introducing a control element at the outset, such as time or number of questions.

After I provided the basic information and answered questions, I told the media when I would be back to talk to them again. "The next briefing will be in one hour, or sooner, if there is a major development," I said.

It is a good idea to let the media know what to expect going forward. Knowing when to expect the next release of information tends to allay their concerns about getting news in a timely manner. The media is very interested, especially during a crisis, in who will be providing the information, when it will be forthcoming and that their competition will not get it before them. Telling them exactly when you will be back addresses all of these concerns.

One hour later, as promised, I briefed the media again, even though there were no new developments. The second briefing was mostly a rehash of what I had said previously. Some might argue that there is no need to talk to the media again until you have new information to disseminate.

However, I believe that during crisis situations, it is important to stay in front of the press on a regular basis. There are many reasons for this, but the most important is that this prevents the spreading of rumor, innuendo and speculation. In a crisis, the media may obtain information from other sources besides the persons who are providing the briefings. This information could come in the form of Tweets or texts (not an issue in 1998) from people who may not have factual information, or even from other reporters whose knowledge may or may not be accurate. If you are not talking to the media on a regular basis to confirm or refute information that they obtain, they may report what they hear without proper verification. If this happens and you are not there to correct it, other stations, so as not to be trumped in reporting a development, may repeat the inaccuracy. It becomes more difficult and time-consuming to set the record straight if this goes on for very long. High visibility and accessibility on the part of the communicator helps mitigate this problem.

At the end of my second briefing, I promised the media I would be back again to talk in one hour. However, I returned much earlier than that. We had a break in the case, and it was big.

The security surveillance video, which showed a grainy image of the backs of two people leaving the hospital, had been put on television by the media soon after I had released it to them in the early hours of the morning. Shortly thereafter, the FBI office in Kansas City received an important phone call. The call was patched to the command post, which had been established at our downtown office.

An FBI agent at the command post called me to pass along the information. "We got a call from an employee at North Kansas City Hospital. They saw the video of the possible suspects that you released to the press," the agent said.

"What about it?" I asked, knowing that there was no way that they could identity anyone from that video, because it didn't show any faces.

"They had two suspicious people in the maternity ward last night," the agent continued. "They were a couple…a man and a woman. They walked around the maternity ward without visiting or talking to anyone."

"Do they have surveillance video? I asked

"They are pulling their tapes now."

A scenario was starting to emerge. The suspects may have been hospital shopping. They went to one hospital, but couldn't get out with a baby, so they tried again at KU, this time with success. It made sense, anyway. The two hospitals are only ten miles apart, and both are very close to the interstate highway, making it easy and quick to get from one to the other. If these were the same people at the other hospital, I knew this was a big break. Certainly they must have better surveillance video. We just couldn't have *two* bad pictures in one case, I concluded.

A little while later, as I sat in my car near the staging area, I got a phone call from the agent. "We have surveillance video," she told me. "It was captured from a camera on the maternity floor."

"Does it show faces?" I asked.

"Yes, man and a woman," she answered.

I asked for six copies of the tape and distributed them to the media as soon as they arrived. It was not long after the news stations aired the video that the FBI command post started receiving phone calls which identified the two persons in the video by name. Other leads were also being checked that led us to the same two people, who were driving their way across the state of Missouri to visit a relative in St. Louis.

A decision was made by the FBI agent in charge of the investigation not to set up roadblocks or stop their vehicle, since this might have presented a danger to Carlie. We knew exactly where the suspects were headed. Once the couple had been identified, the FBI in St. Louis met with relatives of the female suspect at the home where the couple were headed, and found the relatives to be very cooperative. They too wanted to see Carlie returned to her mother. The relatives allowed the agents to wait at their home for the suspects to enter with the baby.

At exactly 10:10 pm, on January 29, 1998, almost twenty-three hours after Carlie was taken from her mother's room at the hospital in Kansas City, Kansas, she was safely recovered and her abductors were arrested without incident at the home in St. Louis. A quick medical appraisal done by a doctor at the scene indicated the baby was in good health.

Shortly after Carlie was recovered, she was taken aboard a private plane and flown to Kansas City. An agent from our office personally delivered the newborn back to the arms of her mother. "That was a once-in-a-lifetime experience," the agent later said.

The subsequent FBI investigation revealed that the motivation for the kidnapping was that the 18-year-old female suspect could not have a baby of her own. In September, 1998, she was sentenced to five years and ten months in federal prison. Her accomplice, 30-year-old man was sentenced to serve more than two years in prison.

The goal of my communication effort with the media in the case of baby Carlie was to provide information that would contribute to her safe recovery and the arrest of the people responsible for her kidnapping. Overall, I believe the effort was successful. A main reason for this success, which provides a lesson for all those in crisis situations, was control. Factors contributing to this control were the establishment of a staging area, which kept the media in one area; regular briefings for the dissemination of information equally to all media outlets on a consistent basis, allowing me to control content and dispel rumors; and my visibility and accessibility as the person in charge of communicating, so that the media knew who would be providing information, how they would get it, and that their competition wouldn't have it before they did. Consideration of all these factors will put the variable of control in your favor and will make it much more likely that a communication effort will be successful.

***

Exactly one year to the day after the kidnapping, we had a party for Carlie. It was not a party to celebrate the anniversary of the kidnapping, but rather a party to celebrate her first birthday. It was also a chance for the more than one hundred agents who had worked so hard on the case to meet the baby they had helped to rescue. The media was invited to the party and *The Kansas City Star* snapped a picture of me holding the baby up in the air. The picture, which was published in the next day's paper, showed me holding the baby, who had the most quizzical look on her face. Looking at the newspaper, I wondered what type of person she would grow up to be and what she would think of all this when she was old enough to understand.

In 2008, shortly before I retired from the FBI, a reporter with *The Kansas City Star* was writing a story about my retirement. When he asked me about the most rewarding case I ever worked on, I didn't hesitate to say it was the case of baby Carlie. The story about my retirement was published with the picture of me holding the baby, taken nine years prior at the baby's first birthday party. That day I received a call from Carlie's mother, who said she had seen the picture of me holding her baby in the newspaper. "She is 10 years old now and in the 4th grade. I have told her all about the kidnapping and I want her to meet you before you retire," she said.

"I would love to see her again, and so would many of the other agents and support employees in our office," I said. After all, I was just one among many that played a role in her recovery.

The day they came to our office was a grand day at the FBI. After several rounds of pictures and introductions to agents and support personnel in the FBI office, I escorted Carlie, her older sister and her mom to the door. I gave all three a long hug. At that moment I was once again thankful that I was able to contribute to her safe recovery by communicating with the media on that cold January morning in 1998. Before the hug was finished, I was also reminded why I joined the FBI twenty years before.

Acknowledgements

Two weeks after being wed to my lovely bride Pam, with her unyielding inspiration and encouragement, we kissed goodbye and I began my training to become an FBI agent. Twenty-three years later, she has continued to provide the support and reassurance that made writing this book possible.

Our son, Christopher continues to amaze me with his quick-witted brand of intelligence. He is talented in so many areas, I find it hard to believe he is from my gene pool. But nonetheless, he has inspired me to find brain power in myself that I wasn't sure existed.

Our daughter Angela's outstanding sense of compassion has touched me profoundly and affected the way I relate to others. I am sure she will apply her kindness someday to make the world a better place.

I would like to thank my parents for the constant support and reassurance they gave me throughout my formative years. They helped me to realize that I could achieve whatever I set my mind to do.

I am grateful to my brothers, Steve, Paul and John, who invigorated my spirits during the difficult weeks of training at Quantico. Their words of encouragement made a big difference at a very important time.

A special mention is for my brother Tommy, the fourth and best-looking of the five Lanza boys. A lovely man of special needs, he has deeply inspired me to appreciate my blessings and apply every ounce of aptitude in all my life's endeavors.

I am deeply appreciative of the help provided by to me in writing this book by two very intelligent women. They are Maggie McCoy, a queen of grammar, and Kerry Philben, an empress of prose. They saw a student in need and patiently applied their powers to drastically improve this text.

Author's Note

Pistols to Press is a memoir of my experience as an FBI Special Agent and spokesman. The book is based on my best recollection of events and dialogue, supported by interviews of colleagues, news accounts, court records and personal notes.

Many of the individuals described in these events are currently employed by the FBI. Their names have been omitted to protect their identity.

About the Author

Jeff Lanza was an FBI Special Agent for over 20 years. He investigated corruption, fraud, organized crime, cyber-crime, human trafficking and terrorism. He has appeared on the Today Show, Good Morning America, Dateline and Larry King Live, among others. He is passionate about keeping people and organizations safe from risk and has presented to thousands around the globe. His clients include many Fortune 500 companies. Jeff loves talking to audiences the world over, but is most comfortable in his home city, where he serves as a certified Kansas City barbeque judge.